the great fights

SO-AZA-839

the great fights

80 epic encounters from the history of boxing

PETER BROOKE-BALL

WITH CONTRIBUTING EDITORS **DEREK O'DELL & O. F. SNELLING**

southwater

This edition is published by Southwater

Southwater is an imprint of
Anness Publishing Limited
Hermes House
88–89 Blackfriars Road
London SE1 8HA
tel. 020 7401 2077
fax 020 7633 9499

Distributed in the UK by
The Manning Partnership
251–253 London Road East
Batheaston
Bath BA1 7RL
tel. 01225 852 727
fax 01225 852 852

Distributed in the USA by
National Books Network
4720 Boston Way
Lanhan
MD 20706
tel. 301 459 3366
fax 301 459 1705

Distributed in Australia by
Sandstone Publishing
Unit 1, 360 Norton Street
Leichhardt
New South Wales 2040
tel. 02 9560 7888
fax 02 9560 7488

All rights reserved. No part of this publication may be reproduced, stored in a retrieval system,
or transmitted in any way or by any means, electronic, mechanical, photocopying, recording
or otherwise, without the prior written permission of the copyright holder.

© 2001 Anness Publishing Limited

Publisher Joanna Lorenz
Project Editors Johnnie Glasses and Felicity Forster
Art Director Peter Bridgewater
Designers Peter Laws and Axis Design
Production Controller Ben Worley

EDITORS' DEDICATION
The editors dedicate this book to all those members of the various EX-BOXERS' ASSOCIATIONS
around the world who do so much for charity with their generosity and enthusiasm.

PRODUCER'S DEDICATION
To John Ringshaw

Previously published as part of a larger volume, *Boxing*.

1 3 5 7 9 10 8 6 4 2

CONTENTS

INTRODUCTION

Above: Primo Carnera (right) in the process of scoring one of his best wins, against Tommy Loughran in their 1934 heavyweight title bout in Miami. Many still look back to the 1920s, 30s and 40s as the heart of boxing's history. The sport was not so highly organized, and the fighters risked greater injury for lower rewards, but there were fewer pointless matches, less hype and hot air, and there was an honest endeavour and grittiness that is often missing today.

Left: Two of the greatest, Thomas Hearns and 'Sugar' Ray Leonard, meet in Las Vegas in 1989 in what was a truly classic encounter. The fight ended in a draw.

Right: Three separate fights are portrayed in this red and black decoration found on a Greek *cylix* (chalice) which is kept in the British Museum. In the top, left, depiction, two boxers, wearing *himantes*, are sparring. The figure to the left is attempting to parry a blow prior to delivering a right uppercut. The two grappling figures appear to have broken the rules by wrestling and are being brought to heel by the referee who holds a forked stick, the symbol of his authority. In the bottom section, two fighters are flailing at each other with open hands under the keen eye of the referee, while the figure to the right prepares a thong prior to wrapping it around his hands.

Until the British resurrected the sport in the early eighteenth century, boxing had remained dormant since the fall of the Roman Empire. Needless to say men, more often than not fortified with ale, had settled matters of honour with fisticuffs in the interim, but not according to any recognized set of rules.

The origins of boxing date back to ancient Greece: Homer mentions a form of organized boxing in the *Iliad*. The honour of 'inventing' the sport, however, goes to the Greek king Theseus, who is thought to have introduced boxing as an entertainment some time before the fifth century BC.

Over the years boxers evolved ways of protecting themselves and, as a consequence, bouts grew longer. They bound their hands with soft leather thongs (*himantes*) not so that they could deliver more punishing blows, nor indeed to soften blows, but so that their knuckles, thumbs and forearms were protected from fractures and grazes.

The rules in ancient Greek boxing were few and far between and mostly relied on traditional codes of honour. For example, punches to any part of the body were permitted but grappling and wrestling were not considered sportsmanlike. There were no rings as such in early forms of boxing, simply fighting areas defined by spectators. This meant that it was difficult for an attacking boxer to pin his man down in a corner, as the besieged fighter could always back away. Ring-craft was virtually non-existent, and the two boxers invariably stood with their feet anchored to one spot as they swung blows at each other. The concept of having 'rounds' did not occur to the Greeks, so the two men continued to slug each other until one surrendered or was knocked senseless.

Boxing was first included in the ancient Olympic Games at the twenty-third Olympiad in 688 BC. There were no weight divisions, so small men stood little chance when exchanging blows with the brawny hulks who invariably ended up as the champions.

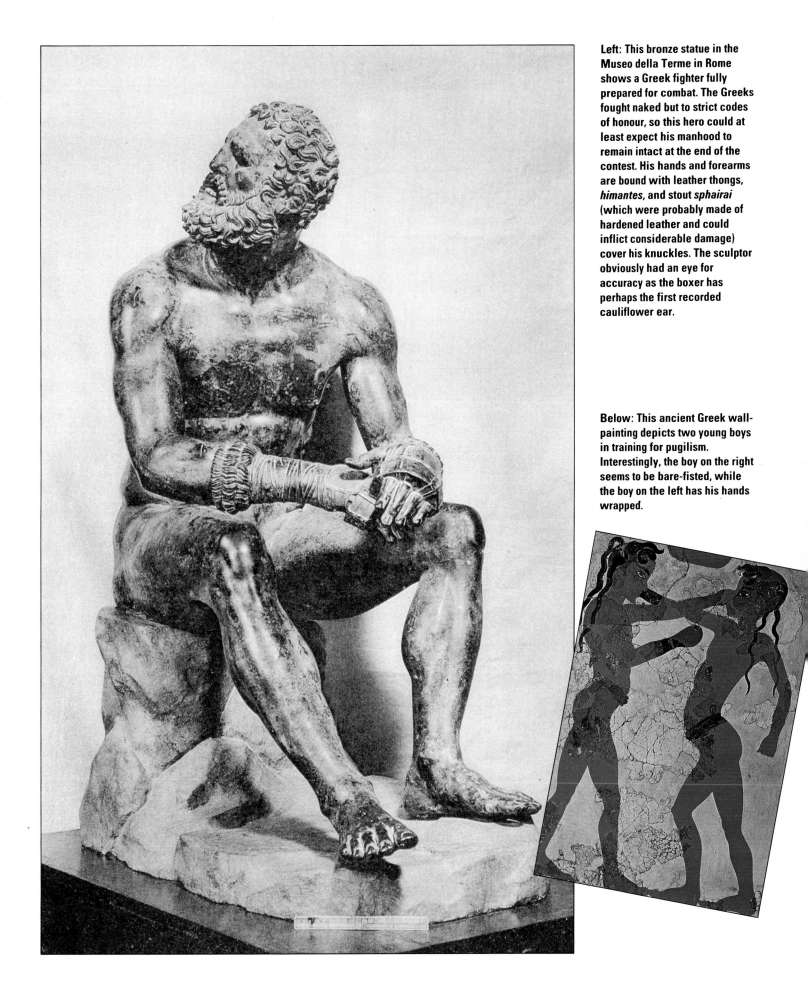

Left: This bronze statue in the Museo della Terme in Rome shows a Greek fighter fully prepared for combat. The Greeks fought naked but to strict codes of honour, so this hero could at least expect his manhood to remain intact at the end of the contest. His hands and forearms are bound with leather thongs, *himantes*, and stout *sphairai* (which were probably made of hardened leather and could inflict considerable damage) cover his knuckles. The sculptor obviously had an eye for accuracy as the boxer has perhaps the first recorded cauliflower ear.

Below: This ancient Greek wall-painting depicts two young boys in training for pugilism. Interestingly, the boy on the right seems to be bare-fisted, while the boy on the left has his hands wrapped.

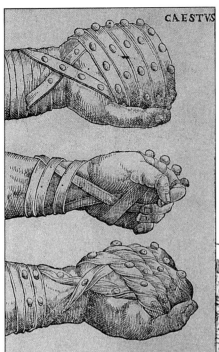

Left: The introduction of the *caestus* by the Romans began the decline of ancient boxing, which thereafter became a gladiatorial sport in which men fought to the death for the amusement of spectators. The *caesti* illustrated here may not be wholly accurate representations of what the weapons actually looked like, as they first appeared as wood engravings in *De Arte Gymnastica*, a book by Hieronymus Mercurialis which was not published until 1573. They do, however, give an impression of how the gruesome implements were worn and what they were fashioned from. Made from leather thongs encrusted with metal beads, the *caestus* was heavy and lethal. The bottom illustration shows twisted thongs which presumably added more cutting power.

Right: This somewhat romantic impression of gladiators fighting in ancient Rome is also taken from a wood-engraved illustration found in *De Arte Gymnastica*. The men wear *caesti*, but both appear to be physically unscathed. In truth, such a contest would have been a bloody affair and one solid punch would have been sufficient to kill or severely maim an opponent. Also missing from the drawing are ranks of spectators baying for blood. It could be that the illustration is supposed to represent fighters in training, but it is highly unlikely that professional gladiators would risk a sparring session while wearing deadly *caesti*.

Left: The decoration on this sixth-century BC vase shows pugilists going hard at each other with *caesti* on their fists.

One bruiser by the name of Milo is said to have won the boxing competition at four consecutive Games. Seventy-two years after boxing was introduced to the Olympics, a junior division for boys was included, and was no doubt used by ambitious youngsters as a stepping stone to gain entry to the senior competition four years later. Contrary to popular belief, Greek athletes at the Olympics were not amateurs but hardened professionals. Sure enough, the victor of a competition was awarded his wreath of bay leaves, but he was also given a prize of 500 drachmas and was entitled to free food for life.

During the latter days of the ancient Olympics, Romans and other foreigners were allowed to take part and so boxing was taken to Rome. By this time, boxers had given up soft wrappings and had taken to wearing hard and sharp *himantes* which were designed to inflict wounds as well as to protect. The ancient Romans, with their notorious lust for blood, were not convinced that the new, improved *himantes* were sufficiently lethal, so they devised the *caestus*.

The *caestus* was a weapon worn by professional gladiators and comprised a binding studded with stones or sharpened spikes of metal. The men who wore these fought for their lives in the circus, fully aware that one blow to the temple would be sufficient to kill. There were no rules in gladiatorial boxing and the sport degenerated into bloody combat, the victor being the one who slaughtered his opponent before he himself was dispatched. Fighters did not know the meaning of self-defence – any boxer who attempted to protect himself would certainly get the thumbs down – and the hapless men were simply trained to absorb punishment and to hit before being hit. The boxing skills which are recognized today, and which the Greeks may have developed before they were over-run, were never given a chance to evolve by the Romans. Gladiators continued to fight in arenas for the amusement of bloodthirsty spectators until the fall of the Roman Empire in the fifth century AD. And when the Empire fell, the sport of boxing, if sport is the right word, disappeared with it.

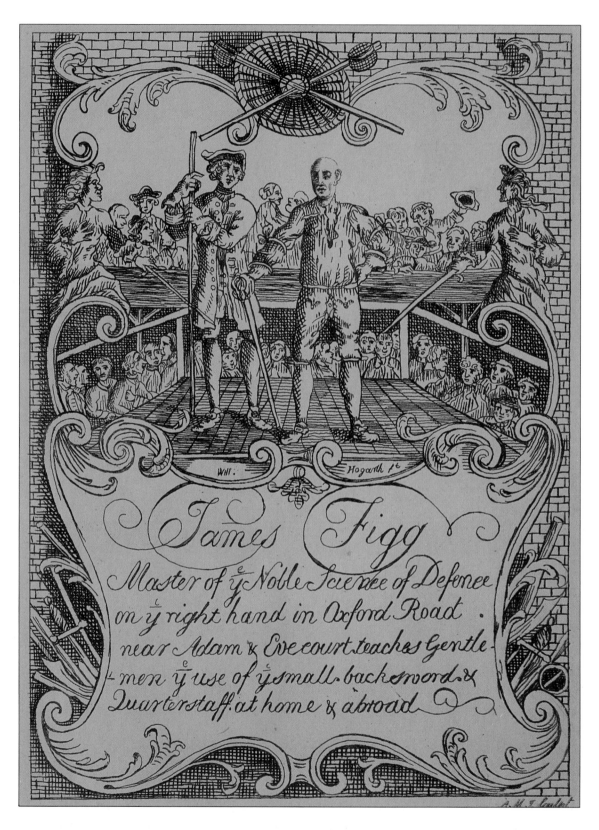

Above: James Figg's card of 1719, which was engraved for him by his friend, the great English painter William Hogarth. This was the first advertisement for the 'Noble Science of Defence'. In addition to boxing, **Figg also taught his clients how to use the sword and the quarterstaff.**

Right: John (Jack) Broughton (1704–1789) is regarded as the 'Father of Boxing'. He established a boxing school and arena near the Haymarket in London, and he encouraged his pupils to wear gloves so that they would not inflict too much damage on each other. After one of his defeated opponents, George Stevenson, died, Broughton introduced a set of rules which remained in force for the best part of a century. He became a Yeoman of the Guard at the Tower of London and there is a memorial to him in Westminster Abbey.

An Englishman by the name of James Figg is credited with the rebirth of boxing, when, in 1719, he advertised a boxing exhibition at his booth at Southwark Fair in London. Figg was known at this time as a cudgel-fighter and swordsman, but he claimed to be boxing's first champion, and went on to open his celebrated amphitheatre in what is now the West End of London. One of Figg's major achievements was to attract the attention of England's gentry. He was lucky to be a friend of the painter William Hogarth, who completed a portrait of Figg, and produced illustrated publicity leaflets for his fights. As well as being the first boxing champion, Figg also became the first promoter.

Figg had many fistic encounters at his amphitheatre, where the arena was surrounded by wooden planks, and he attracted international opposition. He retired undefeated in 1734 and one of his pupils, George Taylor, assumed the title of champion. In 1740, Taylor was beaten by Jack Broughton, who immediately began to revolutionize boxing. Three years later, Broughton built his own amphitheatre, complete with a raised stage, and drafted a set of rules which were to transform the sport. Until Broughton's rules were published, there was no official code of conduct, and a boxer was allowed to use any tactic he wished. Broughton remained champion until 1750, when he was beaten by Jack Slack. However, while Broughton had been hailed as the 'Father of Boxing' and was favoured by the aristocracy, Jack Slack and his contemporaries did little for the sport, and boxing lost favour with the public and its wealthy patrons amid evidence of bribery and corruption.

A new era of bare-knuckle fighting began with the arrival of the Spanish-English Jew, Daniel Mendoza, in 1787. By the middle of the 1800s the sport had taken root in America, but at the end of that century the sport had fallen into disarray once more, especially in England, due to the preachings of the influential clergy. More and more English and Irish boxers spent time in the United States, where the sport continued. Paddy Ryan became the American champion in 1876, but his reign was brief, and he lost his title to the mighty John L. Sullivan. With the coming of Sullivan was born a new breed of fighters, and the first generation of what is known as the modern game.

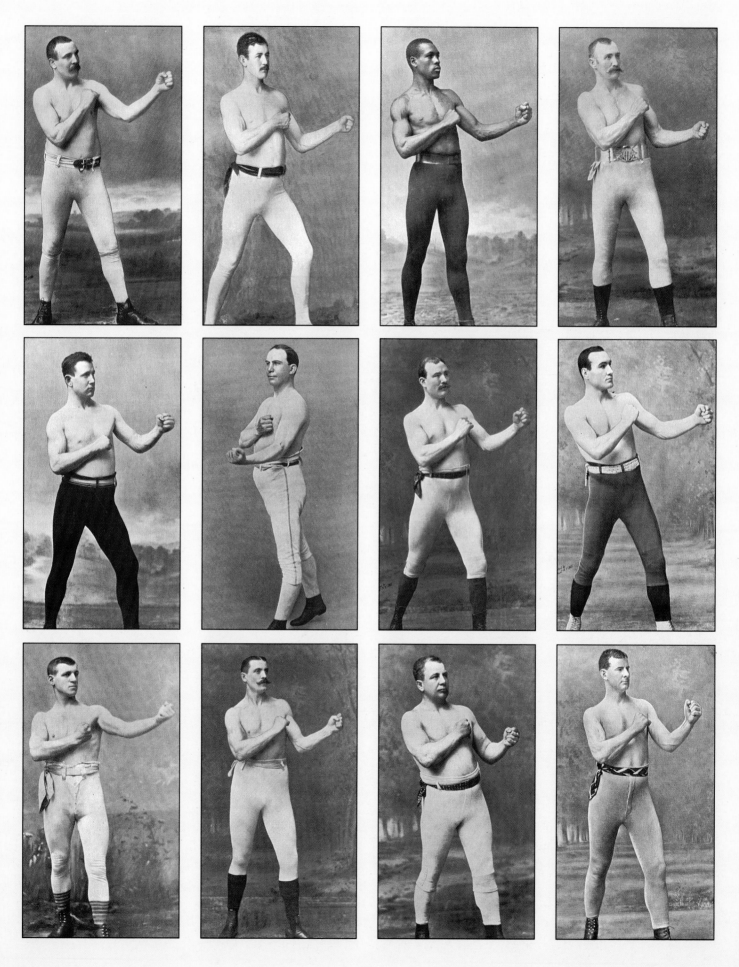

THE BARE-KNUCKLE ERA

On these two pages are shown a host of champions and nearly-men from the 1890s and 1900s – the golden age of the fight game, when bare-fisted sluggers gave way to the modern giants. Smaller pictures: top rank, left to right: Jim Fell; Joe McAuliffe; Frank Craig; Mike Donovan; 'Denver' Ed Smith. Middle rank: Jim Daly; Joe Goss; Jack Welch; Jack Ashton; John Donaldson. Bottom rank: Samuel Blakelock; Captain J C Dailey; William Sheriff; Frank Herald; 'Sparrow' Golden. Above left: Jimmy Carney. Above right: George Godfrey. Right: Jimmy Carroll.

THE RING

RULES

TO BE OBSERVED IN ALL BATTLES ON THE STAGE

I. THAT a fquare of a Yard be chalked in the middle of the Stage; and on every frefh fet-to after a fall, or being parted from the rails, each Second is to bring his Man to the fide of the fquare, and place him oppofite to the other, and till they are fairly fet-to at the Lines, it fhall not be lawful for one to ftrike at the other.

II. That, in order to prevent any Difputes, the time a Man lies after a fall, if the Second does not bring his Man to the fide of the fquare, within the fpace of half a minute, he fhall be deemed a beaten Man.

III. That in every main Battle, no perfon whatever fhall be upon the Stage, except the Principals and their Seconds; the fame rule to be obferved in bye-battles, except that in the latter, Mr. Broughton is allowed to be upon the Stage to keep decorum, and to affift Gentlemen in getting to their places, provided always he does not interfere in the Battle; and whoever pretends to infringe thefe Rules to be turned immediately out of the houfe. Every body is to quit the Stage as foon as the Champions are ftripped, before the fet-to.

IV. That no Champion be deemed beaten, unlefs he fails coming up to the line in the limited time, or that his own Second declares him beaten. No Second is to be allowed to afk his man's Adversary any queftions, or advife him to give out.

V. That in bye-battles, the winning man to have two-thirds of the Money given, which fhall be publicly divided upon the Stage, notwithftanding any private agreements to the contrary.

VI. That to prevent Difputes, in every main Battle the Principals fhall, on coming on the Stage, choofe from among the gentlemen prefent two Umpires, who fhall abfolutely decide all Difputes that may arife about the Battle; and if the two Umpires cannot agree, the faid Umpires to choofe a third, who is to determine it.

VII. That no perfon is to hit his Adverfary when he is down, or feize him by the ham, the breeches, or any part below the waift : a man on his knees to be reckoned down.

As agreed by feveral Gentlemen at Broughton's Amphitheatre,
Tottenham Court Road, Auguft 16, 1743.

DANIEL MENDOZA & RICHARD HUMPHRIES

THE EVOLUTION OF BOXING RULES

When Englishman James Figg opened his London amphitheatre in 1719, effectively heralding the rejuvenation of the sport after more than a thousand years of dormancy, the rules of boxing were rudimentary to say the least. It was not unheard of for a man to have his eyes gouged out or to be 'purred' (kicked while down): and in those days fighters wore spiked boots!

At this time all fights were bare-fisted – nothing was allowed or used to protect the hands. Most fights took place in cordoned-off booths, but in 1723 King George I ordered a square 'ring' to be erected in Hyde Park where anybody could go and spar or fight if they so wished.

In 1741, George Stevenson died of injuries that he had sustained in the ring. The man who beat him, Jack Broughton, was so devastated that he drafted a

Opposite: The first rules of Prize Ring boxing were introduced by Jack Broughton in 1743. Although there is no mention of gloves in the text, the illustrations at the top show fighters wearing 'mufflers' and Broughton encouraged their use at his amphitheatre so that his pupils would be saved 'from the inconveniency of black eyes, broken jaws, and bloody noses'.

Above: Mendoza (left) and 'Gentleman' Richard Humphries fought each other four times, each winning two contests. At their second meeting, in January 1788, they fought for 150 guineas on a twenty-four-foot stage and Humphries got the better of his opponent in twenty-nine minutes. Mendoza became champion in 1792 on beating Bill Ward but lost the crown to 'Gentleman' John Jackson, in 1795.

Right, and below: These two prints illustrate the second Tom Cribb v Tom Molineaux encounter. Cribb had beaten Molineaux in 1810 in thirty-nine rounds and their return match the following year attracted a crowd of some 25,000 to the arena at Thistleton Gap, Leicester. Cribb trained seriously for the fight, reducing his weight from 224 pounds to 188 pounds, and his endeavours paid off: he broke his opponent's jaw in the ninth round and Molineaux failed to get up in the eleventh.

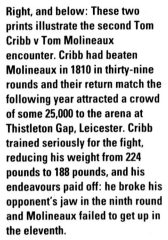

set of rules that effectively governed boxing for nearly a hundred years. Broughton's Rules were hardly extensive, but they were at least a start. He recommended that boxers be brought to a square in the centre of the ring before sparring again after a knockdown; that when a man was knocked down he should be given up to thirty seconds to recover; and that a man should be disqualified if he wrestled below

the belt or hit his opponent when he was down.

In his bid to make boxing safer, Broughton also encouraged the use of 'mufflers' – an early form of boxing-glove. He recommended their use, not for competition fights, but for amateurs and for professionals while training.

Broughton's Rules still left plenty of room for manoeuvre. There was no limit to the number of

rounds a bout should consist of, and individual rounds only ended when a man was knocked to the ground. This explains why some fights lasted for several hours, or were known to continue for more than a hundred rounds. Nor did the great man's ideas outlaw some outrageous tactics. 'Gentleman' John Jackson is said to have beaten Daniel Mendoza in 1795 by using a very ungentlemanly ploy: he held Mendoza's head by the hair while he pounded punches into his face.

Broughton was also instrumental in introducing original skills and basic tactics into boxing. He taught his pupils to block and to retreat when they were being pummelled; until these apparently obvious ideas were introduced, men simply stood up to each other and slugged it out. Both Mendoza and 'Gentleman' Jack advanced these skills: Mendoza was one of the first to appreciate the importance of footwork, and Johnson realized the importance of jabbing.

At the turn of the eighteenth century boxing was in a sorry state with fighters and their backers all but openly taking and offering bribes. In an attempt to

Above: Tom Spring and the Irish champion, Jack Langan, fought for the championship at Worcester racecourse in January 1824. During the second round, one of the stands, holding some 2,000 people, collapsed and the fight was temporarily stopped. When the contest was resumed, it lasted for another seventy-three rounds before Langan was knocked senseless. In their return fight, Spring won again in seventy-seven rounds.

The illustrations on this page originally appeared in *Famous Fights*, and show scenes from the infamous second fight between Thompson and Caunt. Even allowing for the renowned imagination of the *Famous Fights* artists, it is obvious that this was no ordinary encounter. William 'Bendigo' Thompson fought Ben Caunt three times, and each battle was won or lost on a foul. There was no love lost between them, and they were in any case two of the dirtiest boxers in an age in which boxing was not known for its obedience to rules. 'Bendigo' eventually lost this encounter in the seventy-fifth round on a disqualification, when he went to ground without being hit. It was quite normal in this period for as much violence to take place outside the ring as inside it, as can be seen below.

stamp out such behaviour, the Pugilistic Club was formed at 'Gentleman' Jack's home in London in 1814. For a time this club was influential in sponsoring and organizing contests, and it called upon ring officials to wear special uniforms so that they could at least be noticed.

When 'Brighton Bill' died after his battle with Owen Swift in 1838, the Pugilists' Protective Association issued a new set of rules, the so-called London Prize Ring Rules, which were intended to make boxing safer still. However even these did not limit

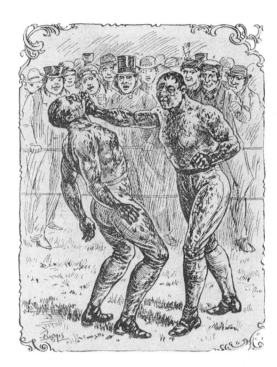

On this page are shown scenes from the match arranged after Tom Sayers, a rising star, was challenged to a fight by Harry Paulson in 1856. What followed was one of the bloodiest of battles, lasting no less than 109 rounds. Both men had been knocked to the floor many times, and both were drenched in blood, when Sayers finally delivered the finishing punch after three hours and eight minutes.

the number of rounds in a bout and a round still lasted until a man was knocked down. The Prize Ring Rules were subsequently revised in 1853 and 1866, largely to catch out such tricksters as 'Bendigo' Thompson and 'Deaf 'Un' Burke who would use any ruse or deceit to win a contest, including head-butting and attempting to throttle an opponent. The Prize Ring Rules also replaced Broughton's square in the middle of the ring with a 'scratch' line at which the two contestants had to face up to each other (hence the term 'up to scratch').

By this time boxing was actively outlawed in England and many fights were broken up by that early version of the modern police force, the Bow Street Runners. Consequently most contests took place in the remote countryside beyond the reach of the law: boxing's word-of-mouth network still ensured considerable audiences. To this day boxing has never been officially legalized in England: it is permitted through a loophole in legislation because it can be described and considered as an 'exhibition of skill'.

In 1866 the Marquess of Queensberry, together

The illustrations on this page show the highlights from the Sayers v Paddock championship match in 1858. Paddock had disputed Sayers' right to the belt (which was then the champion's trophy), and a match was arranged for June 16 to settle the affair. Paddock had been dangerously ill with a fever, but was still heavily backed because of his size: he weighed in at over 170 pounds, while Sayers was under 150. Sayers started strongly, and things looked bad for Paddock after twenty minutes. Then Paddock's main backer and best friend, Alec Keene, with whom he had quarrelled, stepped into the ring to make up their differences (top), and this, together with Keene's tactical advice, gave Paddock the motivation to come back powerfully. But it was not to be for the challenger: drained of energy by his recent fever, he faded after a tremendous effort, and Sayers bested him after a brutal one hour and twenty minutes.

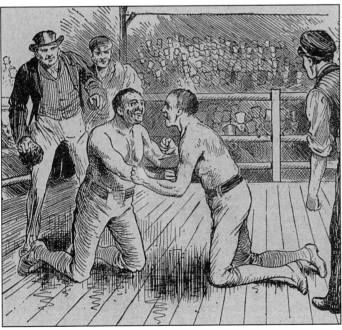

The group of artists' impressions on this page graphically illustrates, even allowing a due degree of scepticism about the lurid quality of the fight pictures of the time, the state of boxing in the early and mid-nineteenth century. Gouging, scratching, kicking, wrestling and butting were quite normal, and the fighters were expected by their backers, who had wagered huge sums, to fight on virtually to the death before quitting.

with Lord Lonsdale and Arthur Chambers, issued new rules which completely revolutionized boxing. The so-called Queensberry Rules had twelve clauses, the most important being: *a*) a ring should be twenty-four feet square, *b*) that wrestling should be illegal, *c*) that rounds should last for three minutes and that there should be a one-minute break between rounds, and *d*) that gloves should be worn. The rules were subsequently revised to limit the number of rounds to twenty, and the minimum weight for gloves was regulated to six ounces. A scoring system was also

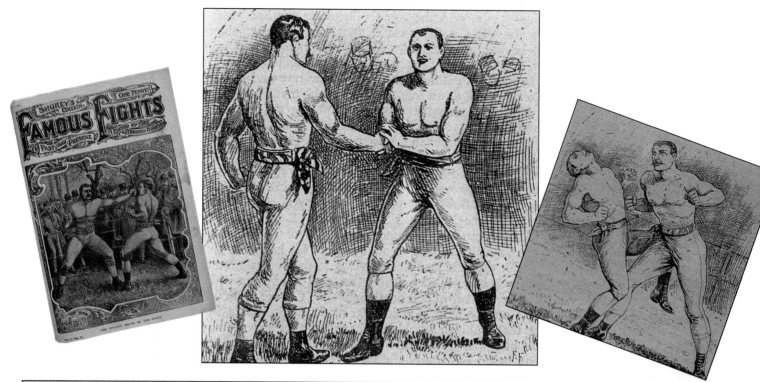

One of the last and most famous bare-knuckle contests was fought out between the American hero, John L Sullivan (with moustache), and England's Charlie Mitchell on March 10 1888, highlights of which are illustrated, left. The venue for the encounter was Chantilly, in France, and the world title was at stake. After thirty-nine rounds and three hours and ten minutes of combat, the contest was declared a draw because of the muddy conditions. After the fight both men were arrested and were obliged to nurse their heavy heads in police cells. On the right is shown the magnificent physique of Charlie Mitchell, champion of England. He boxed on after his defeat by Sullivan, with great success, and eventually challenged James J Corbett for the championship of the world on January 25 1894 at the Duval Athletic Club, Jacksonville, Florida. A phenomenal purse of $20,000 was put up, but Mitchell was soundly and brutally dispatched in the third round.

introduced, with each combatant being awarded points according to his performance.

Queensberry's rules did not catch on immediately and bare-knuckle fighting continued to take place until the turn of the century: the last heavyweight bare-knuckle title fight took place in 1889 between John L Sullivan and Jake Kilrain. Gradually, however, the sense in Queensberry's rules prevailed, and even the likes of Sullivan accepted them (ironically Sullivan lost his first fight under the Queensberry Rules, against James J Corbett).

The concept of weight categories was first mooted in the 1850s and there were originally three divisions: heavyweight (over 156 pounds), middleweight (up to 156 pounds) and lightweight (up to 133 pounds). As boxing grew increasingly popular under the Queens-

berry Rules, more divisions were gradually introduced: there were nine divisions in 1910 and there are no less than seventeen today.

Several important organizations such as the Amateur Boxing Association (in 1880), the Pelican Club (in 1890), and the National Sporting Club (in 1909) adopted and revised the Queensberry Rules in England, and the powerful International Boxing Union (IBU) was created in Paris in 1910. In the United States, the New York State Athletic Commission was established in 1920 and did much to publicize the 'new' sport, which really boomed in the period between the two world wars.

In Britain the welfare of professional boxers was overseen by the British Boxing Board of Control (BBBofC), and around the world a number of new

Above: The last bare-knuckle fight for the world championship was held between John L Sullivan and Jake Kilrain. The fight took place at Richburg, Mississippi on July 8 1889, with Sullivan emerging victorious after seventy-five rounds. The fight marked the end of one era and the dawn of another in more ways than one. This is thought to be the earliest photograph of a boxing match and shows the two men in a clinch during the seventh round.

Far left, and left: These two images of Jake Kilrain at the time of the Sullivan fight emotively illustrate the ending of the early years and the beginning of the modern age. At the same time that the rules were recodified, and gloves became standard for all fights, the charming and imaginative woodcut images of the great fights and famous boxers were finally superseded by the new art of photography.

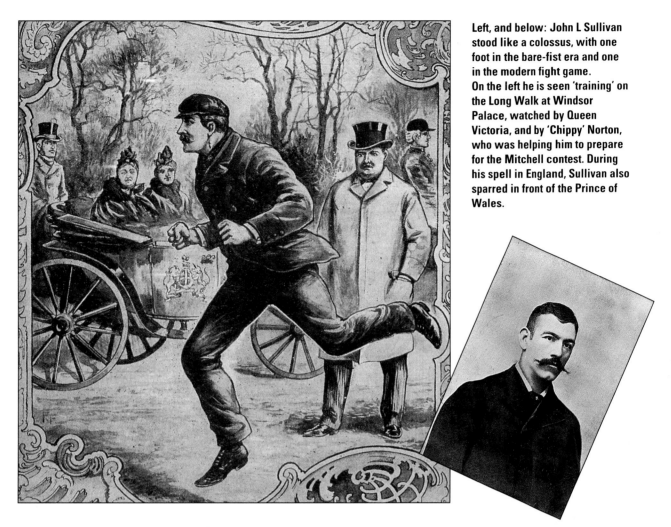

Left, and below: John L Sullivan stood like a colossus, with one foot in the bare-fist era and one in the modern fight game. On the left he is seen 'training' on the Long Walk at Windsor Palace, watched by Queen Victoria, and by 'Chippy' Norton, who was helping him to prepare for the Mitchell contest. During his spell in England, Sullivan also sparred in front of the Prince of Wales.

regulatory bodies began to spring up. Unfortunately they more often than not squabbled with one another about their areas of responsibility and a large degree of chaos, which has never been resolved, ensued. In the United States, the National Boxing Association (NBA) was formed in 1921 in opposition to the New York Athletic Association, which had effectively monopolized championship boxing up until then. By the 1930s there were State champions, New York champions, NBA champions and IBU champions, each of whom frequently claimed that they held the world title. It was only when the various claimants fought each other that a genuine and undisputed world champion emerged.

The IBU became the European Boxing Union (EBU) in 1946 and the NBA changed its name to the World Boxing Association (WBA) in 1962. Despairing at the arrogance of the WBA, the BBBofC, several American state organizations, the EBU and various other governing bodies combined to create the World Boxing Council (WBC) in 1963. Numerous attempts were made to unify the WBA with the WBC,

but to no avail. In fact worse was to follow. In 1983 the International Boxing Federation (IBF) was formed, and in 1988 the World Boxing Organization (WBO) was created. Consequently it is now possible to have four world champions in each of the seventeen weight divisions. Many believe that this fragmentation has done much to devalue titles and diffuse interest in boxing in the last two decades.

Today boxing rules for professionals vary only marginally between the various different organizations (and all are based on the Queensberry Rules). For example, a professional bout can last for eight rounds or twelve; a round can be two minutes long or three; the referee can be the sole arbiter, or a panel of three independent judges can be used.

Amateur boxing has taken its own route, and by and large the rules for the amateur game are much more stringent than those used for professional contests. Rounds can last two or three minutes but there are usually only three rounds in a bout. It is normal now for amateurs to wear head-guards in their fights, in addition to their traditional vests.

LANDMARKS IN BOXING HISTORY

James Figg v Ned Sutton, 1720
Figg defeats Sutton to become the first recognized champion of England.

'Gentleman' John Jackson v Daniel Mendoza; April 15 1795; Hornchurch, Essex.
Jackson beats Mendoza in ten and a half minutes for a purse of 100 guineas, heralding a new age of 'scientific' boxing.

Tom Cribb v Tom Molineaux; December 10 1810; Copthall Common.
The first title fight in which a black person was involved. The two fought for 200 guineas a side plus 100 guineas prize money. Cribb won in fifty-five minutes (thirty-nine rounds).

Tom Cribb v Tom Molineaux; September 28 1811; Thistleton Gap, Leicester.
An estimated crowd of 25,000 turned out to watch this rematch for a prize of 600 guineas.

Cribb won again in twenty minutes (eleven rounds).

Jacob Hyer v Tom Beasley; 1816; New York.
The first American fight that was open to the public. Hyer won and claimed the American championship.

Tom Spring v Jack Langan; January 7 1824;
The first title fight for which a grandstand was built; an estimated 30,000 watched. Spring won in two hours twenty minutes (seventy-five rounds).

James 'Deaf 'Un' Burke v Simon Byrne; May 30 1833; No-Man's-Land, Hertfordshire.
The longest title fight on record, lasting three hours six minutes (ninety-nine rounds). Burke won, and Byrne later died of his horrific injuries.

Tom Sayers (Eng) v John C Heenan (USA); April 17 1860; Farnborough Common.
The first international world championship fight.

The contest, for £200 a side, ended in chaos and was declared a draw after two hours six minutes (thirty-seven rounds).

Jack 'Nonpareil' Dempsey (Ire) v George Fulljames (Can); July 30 1884; Staten Island, New York.
Dempsey becomes the first world champion (middleweight) fighting to Queensberry Rules. He knocked out Fulljames in the twenty-second round.

John L Sullivan (USA) v Jake Kilrain (USA); July 8 1889; Richburg, Mississippi.
The last heavyweight title

fight to be fought with bare knuckles. Sullivan won the $10,000 a side contest in seventy-five gruelling rounds.

John L Sullivan (USA) v James J Corbett (USA); September 7 1892; New Orleans.
Corbett becomes the first heavyweight world champion under the Queensberry Rules. He knocked out Sullivan in the twenty-first round to gain $45,000.

Jack Dempsey (USA) v Georges Carpentier (Fr); July 2 1921; New Jersey.
The first fight to gross more than $1 million at the gate ($1,789,238). Dempsey knocked out Carpentier in four rounds to retain the world heavyweight title.

'Marvelous' Marvin Hagler (USA) v 'Sugar' Ray Leonard (USA); April 6 1987; Las Vegas.
The richest fight in boxing history. Gross takings for the fight are thought to have exceeded $100 million; Hagler pocketed $17 million of the $28 million purse and Leonard $11 million. Leonard won the middleweight contest on a split decision.

Opposite page: First column; Mendoza smashes a left into the chin of 'Gentleman' John Jackson, but Jackson came back to win very quickly. Second column; John C Heenan tried to avoid capture after the break-up of his fight with Sayers, but was eventually taken into custody. Third column, top; *Famous Fights* illustrated the boxers' fists in their coverage of the 1860 fight – Sayers' above, and Heenan's below. Third column, middle; Jack Dempsey, 'The Nonpareil', in shape for his 1884 battle against George Fulljames.

Left: Weight divisions were not devised until the middle of the nineteenth century. This print shows Thomas Johnson (left) fighting Isaac Perrins in 1789.

WEIGHT DIVISIONS

Heavyweight	unlimited		**Featherweight** (WBC super-bantamweight)	up to 126 pounds
Cruiserweight	up to 190 pounds		**Junior-featherweight** (WBC super-bantamweight)	up to 122 pounds
Light-heavyweight	up to 175 pounds		**Bantamweight**	up to 118 pounds
Super-middleweight	up to 168 pounds		**Junior-bantamweight** (WBC super-flyweight)	up to 115 pounds
Middleweight	up to 160 pounds		**Flyweight**	up to 112 pounds
Junior-middleweight (WBC super-welterweight)	up to 154 pounds		**Junior-flyweight** (WBC light-flyweight)	up to 108 pounds
Welterweight	up to 147 pounds		**Straw-weight** (IBF and WBA Mini-flyweight)	up to 105 pounds
Junior-welterweight (WBC super-lightweight)	up to 140 pounds			
Lightweight	up to 135 pounds			
Junior-lightweight (WBC super-featherweight)	up to 130 pounds			

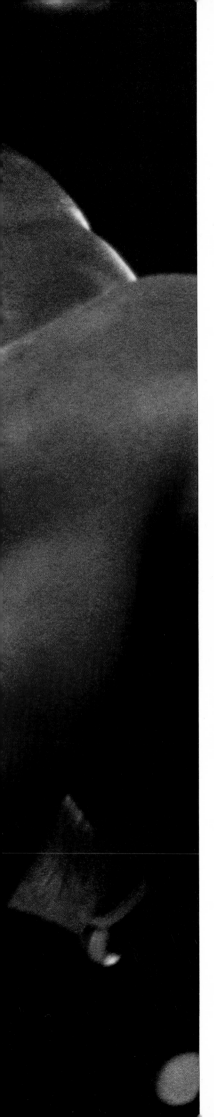

THE GLOVED ERA

Above: Ted 'Kid' Lewis charges in against Johnny Basham at the Royal Albert Hall, London, on November 19 1920, in their second fight. The European title was at stake, and was retained by Lewis when he knocked out the courageous Basham in the nineteenth round.

Left: Bruno and Tyson exchange blows in their 1989 heavyweight title bout. Although this was 'just another championship fight' in world terms, it was an emotional contest for British fans, and Bruno did more than expected before Tyson came through with the heavy guns to stop him in the fifth round.

PETER MAHER V BOB FITZSIMMONS

February 21 1896
near Langtry, Texas

Above: Peter Maher was born in County Galway, Ireland, in 1868. He fought his way to the championship nomination with famous victories over Gus Lambert, 'Bubbles' Davis, Jim Daly, Jack Fallon, 'Sailor' Brown and George Godfrey. He had previously lost to Fitzsimmons in New Orleans on March 2 1892.

Below: The unusual shape of Bob Fitzsimmons.

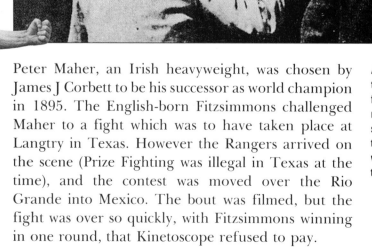

Peter Maher, an Irish heavyweight, was chosen by James J Corbett to be his successor as world champion in 1895. The English-born Fitzsimmons challenged Maher to a fight which was to have taken place at Langtry in Texas. However the Rangers arrived on the scene (Prize Fighting was illegal in Texas at the time), and the contest was moved over the Rio Grande into Mexico. The bout was filmed, but the fight was over so quickly, with Fitzsimmons winning in one round, that Kinetoscope refused to pay.

Above: Fitzsimmons (right) about to finish off Maher with his famous left hook in the opening round. In the background can be seen enthusiastic Mexicans who turned up to view the fight which was unexpectedly fought on their territory.

JAMES J CORBETT V BOB FITZSIMMONS

March 17 1897
Carson City, Nevada

Obliged to come out of retirement to defend his world title against Fitzsimmons, Corbett was the hot favourite to win the challenge. The champion had the best of the opening rounds but during the thirteenth, Fitzsimmons' wife yelled 'Hit 'im in the slats, Bob.' Fitzsimmons did just that and floored Corbett in the fourteenth with a punishing blow to the solar plexus. Unable to get up, Corbett finally relinquished his world title.

Top left, Corbett, and top right, Fitzsimmons, as weighed and measured by *Famous Fights* prior to their epic encounter. Far right: The fight was a subject of speculation for months, and the boxing magazines were full of anticipation and profiles.

Right: Corbett (right) leaves his midriff vulnerable; it was a body-blow slipping through just such a defensive weakness that ended his reign as champion.

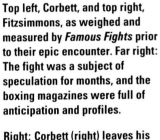

BOB FITZSIMMONS V JAMES J JEFFRIES

June 9 1899
Coney Island, New York

Fitzsimmons lost his world heavyweight title to Jeffries in his first defence, being knocked out in eleven rounds. A return match in 1902 ended in similar fashion.

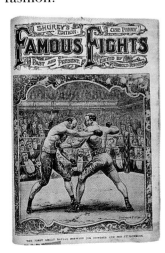

Right: Jeffries shakes hands with the balding Fitzsimmons before the contest.

Left: Cameramen were now in regular attendance at title fights, and this was one of the last fights to be covered by press artists. From here on, the truth of photography would replace the romanticism of the pen and brush.

JOE GANS V 'BATTLING' NELSON

September 3 1906
Goldfield, Nevada

In an epic contest that lasted forty-two rounds, Gans successfully defended his world lightweight title against the Dane, Nelson, who was disqualified. In two subsequent bouts, however, Nelson emerged victorious.

Top left: Joe Gans is thought by many to be the greatest lightweight who ever lived. He was born on November 25 1874 in Philadelphia, and died of consumption on August 10 1910.
Top right: A later portrait of 'Battling' Nelson.

Left: The two boxers shake hands before their second fight in 1908. Nelson won on a knockout.

Below: Despite having consumption, the stylish Gans outboxed 'The Durable Dane'.

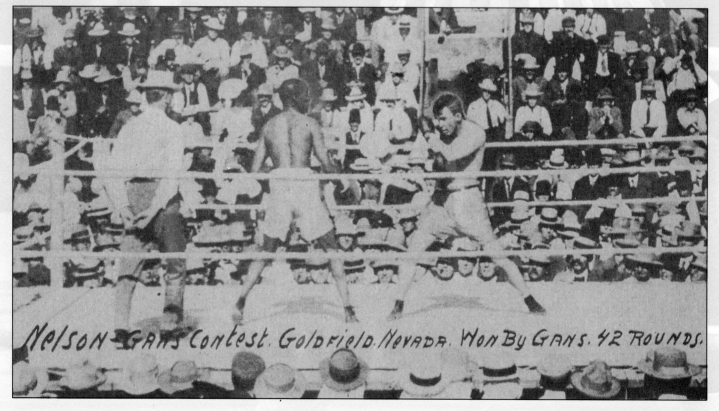

Nelson-Gans Contest. Goldfield. Nevada. Won By Gans. 42 Rounds.

TOMMY BURNS V
JACK JOHNSON

December 26 1908
Sydney, Australia

Johnson was forced to follow Burns all the way to Australia to secure a title fight. He verbally riled the Canadian heavyweight remorselessly throughout the contest and became world champion when the bout was stopped in the fourteenth round.

Top left: The immortal Jack Johnson.

Above: The arrogant Johnson toyed with Burns during the fight, and the clinches gave him the opportunity to taunt the champion with abuse.

Left: The two boxers being introduced to the crowd with Burns standing on the left.

JACK JOHNSON V
STANLEY KETCHEL

October 16 1909
Colma, California

Johnson's first defence of his world heavyweight title was against the 'Great White Hope', Ketchel. An agreement was reached beforehand whereby the contest would end in a draw, thus ensuring a lucrative rematch. However, when Ketchel floored him early in the twelfth round, Johnson immediately retaliated in lethal fashion and knocked the challenger out cold.

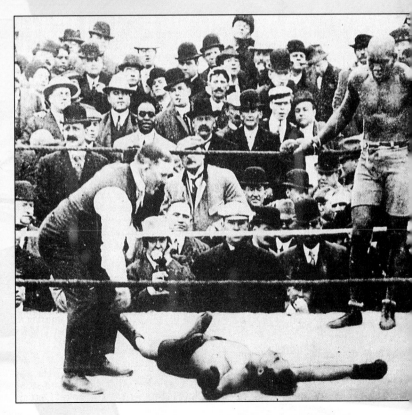

Right: Ketchel takes the count as the infuriated champion looks on.

Left: The extraordinary Stanley Ketchel. He was shot one year after this fight, on October 15 1910, by a jealous rival in love, Walter A Dipley, when aged only twenty-five.

JACK JOHNSON V JAMES J JEFFRIES

July 4 1910
Reno, Nevada

Jeffries, a former heavyweight champion, was hauled out of retirement to take on Johnson. Many racists in the United States could not come to terms with the idea of a black heavyweight title holder, and were desperate for a white champion to put Johnson 'in his place'. But Jeffries was no longer the boxer he once was, and the hopes of the bigots were dashed when the fight was stopped in the fifteenth round.

Left: Foolish money and racist hopes made Jeffries the bookmaker's favourite before the fight, but from the start it was obviously a lost cause. Above: The referee holds back the champion, who is keen to go in for the kill. Right: A familiar pose for Johnson, who towers gloating above his fallen opponent, having taunted him throughout.

JACK JOHNSON V JESS WILLARD

April 5 1915
Havana, Cuba

Johnson finally met his match in Jess Willard, a huge cowboy from Kansas. Johnson controlled most of the fight but, aged thirty-seven and out of condition, he began to wilt under the intense sunlight and was knocked out in the twenty-sixth round.

Right: Johnson (left) was overweight when he fought Willard, and the younger, fitter man was more able to cope with the stifling heat.

Left: Jess Willard was born on December 29 1883 in Pottawatomie County. He held the world title for four years before losing to Dempsey.

Right: Between grim portraits of Dempsey (left) and Willard, Dempsey can be seen launching a ferocious assault on the champion.

Left: These are the last few moments of Willard's tenure of the heavyweight championship. Dempsey (left) unleashes a flurry of blows that pin Willard in a corner. Willard retired on his stool between rounds three and four, saying that he could not go on. The former champion later learned that his jaw had been broken in two places, that he had six broken ribs and that he had lost six of his teeth.

Right: Dempsey in training. Perhaps sensing that this might be his last fight, Willard demanded, and got, a $100,000 fee from Tex Rickard. Dempsey received $27,500, but his big paydays were still to come. Dempsey wagered his whole purse that he would knock out Willard in the first: he very nearly won his bet.

JESS WILLARD V
JACK DEMPSEY

July 4 1919
Toledo, Ohio

Willard was out of shape when he met the trim Jack Dempsey and the challenger was the hot favourite to win. The experts were proved right and Willard retired in the third round after taking a terrible beating.

Jack Dempsey v Georges Carpentier

July 2 1921
Jersey City, New Jersey

In a fight promoted by the great Tex Rickard, and which grossed more than a million dollars at the gate, Dempsey, the world heavyweight champion, was pitted against the popular French war hero, Carpentier, who was the light-heavyweight title holder. The gallant Frenchman broke his thumb in the second round and was counted out in the fourth.

Top left: Even in a posed shot, Dempsey looks threatening. After his victory over Willard, he successfully defended twice, firstly against his friend and sparring partner Billy Miske, on September 6 1920, and then against Bill Brennan, on December 14 1920. He then became embroiled in a scandal over draft evasion in the First World War, for which he was indicted by a Federal Grand Jury. Enterprising as ever, Rickard made this a promotional feature of the Carpentier fight, casting the French war hero against the American draft dodger to drum up rivalry and excitement.

Top right: The Frenchman manages to look debonair even without his three-piece suit and button-hole orchid.

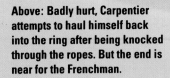

Above: Badly hurt, Carpentier attempts to haul himself back into the ring after being knocked through the ropes. But the end is near for the Frenchman.

GEORGES CARPENTIER V 'BATTLING' SIKI

September 24 1922
Paris, France

Carpentier lost his light-heavyweight title to the little-known Senegalese in one of the major upsets in boxing history. The Frenchman was knocked out in the sixth round.

Below: Carpentier has to be lifted to his feet after being levelled by a stunning punch from Siki in the sixth round.

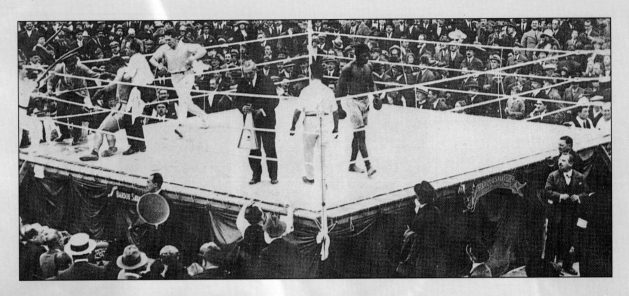

'BATTLING' SIKI V MIKE MCTIGUE

March 17 1923
Dublin

Siki lost his light-heavyweight title to McTigue in his first defence. Performing on his home turf in Dublin, and backed by a chanting Irish crowd on St Patrick's Day, McTigue won on points after twenty rounds.

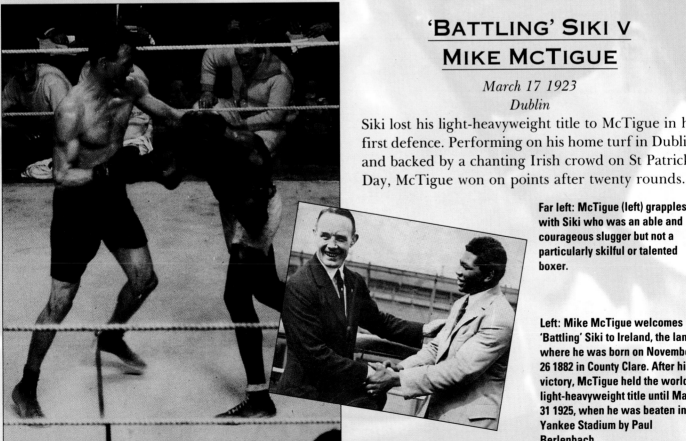

Far left: McTigue (left) grapples with Siki who was an able and courageous slugger but not a particularly skilful or talented boxer.

Left: Mike McTigue welcomes 'Battling' Siki to Ireland, the land where he was born on November 26 1882 in County Clare. After his victory, McTigue held the world light-heavyweight title until May 31 1925, when he was beaten in Yankee Stadium by Paul Berlenbach.

GEORGES CARPENTIER V TED 'KID' LEWIS

May 11 1922
Olympia, London

Right: Ted 'Kid' Lewis.

Below: Carpentier (left) turning Lewis into the path of a left hook.

In a brief, ill-tempered catchweights contest, the pride of France controversially knocked out the smaller, but highly popular, Ted 'Kid' Lewis in the opening round. Lewis, who would fight any man alive, was determined to get Carpentier out of the way and then force heavyweight champion Jack Dempsey into fighting him! At the bell, Lewis tore into the attack. There was holding and wrestling on both sides and some illegal use of the elbows, and the referee was forced to issue several warnings to the contestants. Lewis was rattling the Frenchman and moved inside where he reddened Carpentier's ribs with heavy punches from both hands. The referee moved between the men and again issued a caution for holding. Lewis turned his head briefly to protest and left his chin unguarded for just about as long as it takes to blink. Carpentier, always a great opportunist, saw his chance and swung a right that zeroed on to the target. Lewis crashed to the canvas with no chance of beating the count. The ensuing controversy has continued to the present day.

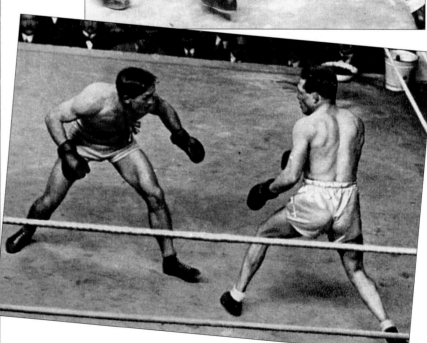

Below: Georges Carpentier knocks out Kid Lewis.

Below right: Carpentier (left) and Lewis spar for an opening.

JACK DEMPSEY V TOMMY GIBBONS

July 4 1923
Shelby, Montana

The business organizations of Shelby have, in recent years, denied that this fight broke any of their banks but it cannot be denied that they lost a lot of money. Tommy Gibbons boxed gallantly for fifteen rounds only to be informed that disappointing gate receipts left nothing in the kitty for him. The town had gambled that a heavy-weight title fight would attract business investment, but rumours that the fight had been cancelled, plus the isolation of the venue, made it a box-office flop. Dempsey's manager demanded, and got, the champion's slice of the purse before getting in the ring. All this detracted from a fine performance on the part of Tommy Gibbons, who became the first man to force the feared champion to travel the fifteen round course. Gibbons, a proud and durable battler, was stopped just once and that was by Gene Tunney in what was Tommy's last fight.

Below: Tommy Gibbons was the only contender to last the distance with Jack. He is shown landing a terrific left to Jack's body in one of the three rounds he was credited with winning.

Above: Tommy Gibbons and Jack Dempsey (right).

Right: Gibbons' left makes contact with Dempsey's jaw.

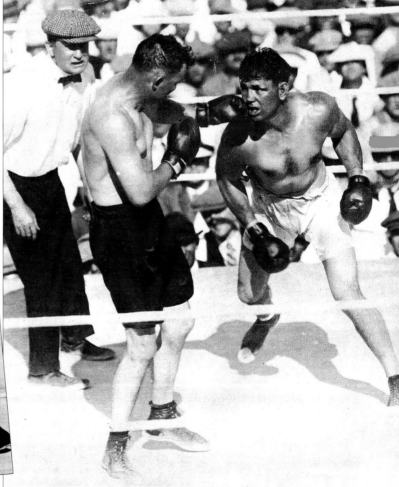

Right: A famous portrait of Dempsey (left), and a handsome picture of the brooding Argentinian. In between, things do not look quite so attractive, as the South American lays flat out on the canvas and Dempsey lounges in a neutral corner.

JACK DEMPSEY V LUIS ANGEL FIRPO

September 14 1923
New York

In one of the most exciting heavyweight contests of all time, Dempsey put his title on the line against Firpo, an Argentinian giant. The contest only lasted two rounds but in that time Firpo was knocked down nine times and Dempsey twice. The champion also had to endure the indignity of being knocked clean through the ropes before rallying to deliver the *coup de grâce*.

Above: Seen from the other side of the ring, things look no better for Firpo. In this most amazing contest, both fighters were knocked down, but in truth Dempsey looks little bothered by affairs, and it was Firpo who soaked up the real punishment. Nevertheless, he lives on in legend as the man who knocked Dempsey out of the ring. Left: Firpo lived a long and contented life. He died a millionaire in August 1960.

GENE TUNNEY V JACK DEMPSEY

September 22 1927
Chicago

Gene Tunney won the world heavyweight title from Jack Dempsey by outpointing the champion in 1926. The return match a year later has become one of the most famous in boxing history and has been dubbed the 'Battle of the Long Count'. Tunney was floored by Dempsey in the seventh round but the challenger failed to retreat to a neutral corner and the seconds that elapsed before the referee started the count were enough to enable Tunney to recover. He retained his title by winning the ten-round bout on points.

Above: The seventh round. Dempsey clips Tunney with a right hook and the champion slumps to the canvas.

Right: The referee (extreme left) instructs Dempsey to retreat to a neutral corner so that he can commence the count over the floored Tunney, but the challenger lingers a while to eye his foe.

Left: With Dempsey (left) in a corner, the referee starts the count but by this time Tunney is on his way up. The champion was said to be down for fourteen seconds – but it is the referee's count that matters.

Far left: Clean-cut ex-Marine Gene Tunney was every mother's dream: he retired as undefeated champion in 1928, and became a highly successful businessman.

JACK SHARKEY V MAX SCHMELING

June 12 1930
New York

Above: Max Schmeling. The retirement of Tunney ended what many still think of as the golden age of gloved boxing. No obvious champion immediately emerged, so there was a succession of eliminators involving many little-known and little-regarded boxers: this process did not catch the imagination of the fight fans. The long-awaited contest between Schmeling and Sharkey to settle the heavyweight crown after nearly two years came as a relief. In the end, the fight was both a disappointment and a sensation: it was a let-down because it lasted only four rounds, and ended in confusion; and a sensation because it was resolved on a foul – the fight being awarded to a groggy Schmeling when his manager, Joe Jacobs, and the famous reporter Arthur Brisbane drew the unsighted referee's attention to Sharkey's killer low blow. Sharkey had already gained a reputation for hitting low against British champion Phil Scott on February 28 of the same year in the final eliminator: Scott always claimed that Sharkey's low punching cost him a shot at the title.

Sharkey and Schmeling were matched against each other for the vacant world heavyweight title. When Sharkey punched the German below the belt towards the end of the fourth round, the German's manager claimed a foul and the referee agreed, so the title was won, but in a most unsatisfactory fashion. As fate would have it, Schmeling lost the title to Sharkey two years later on a controversial points decision.

Above: Schmeling takes a count with Sharkey watching from a neutral corner. The German won the title on a disputed foul after the intervention of his manager, Joe Jacobs.

MAX SCHMELING V MICKEY WALKER

September 26 1932
New York

Chasing heavyweight glory, the former middleweight world champion Mickey Walker took on Schmeling, who had lost his world title to Jack Sharkey three months earlier. It was a bad mistake: the 'Toy Bulldog' took a heavy hammering and failed to come out for the ninth round.

Left: Walker (left) clips Schmeling on the chin in the third round but the 'Toy Bulldog' was himself on the receiving end for most of the fight.

Below: Walker tumbles to the canvas in the eighth round and Schmeling suggests that it might be time for the referee to stop the contest. Walker failed to come out for the ninth.

Primo Carnera v Max Baer

June 14 1934
Long Island

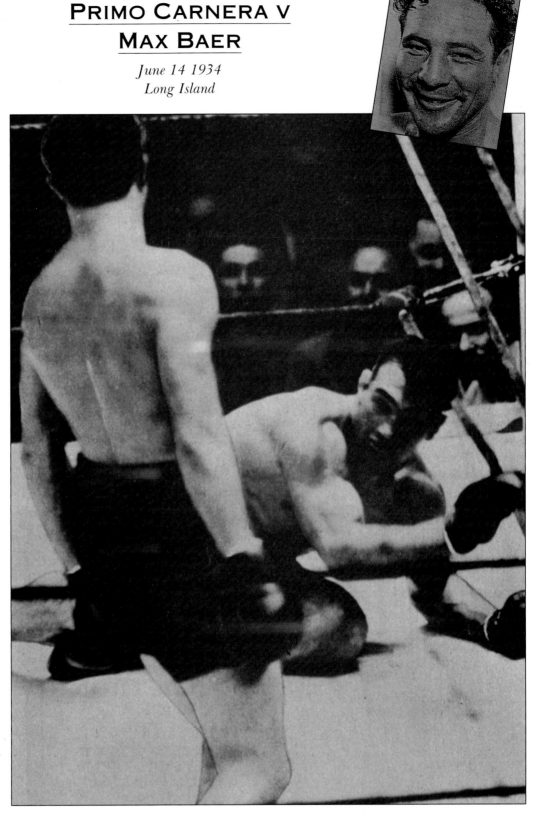

Top left and top right: A full view of Max Baer's fighting form, and a typically cheery portrait. Baer missed being among the very greatest only because he could not focus on the seriousness of what he was doing. He had all the talents required, but loved the good life too much. This win against Carnera was a superb highlight in a dashing and crowd-pleasing career. Above: Here he is dwarfed by Carnera at the weigh-in, standing on the scales to match up their heights. Note the Italian's dapper two-tone shoes and elegant sock suspenders – he was a fashion giant as well.

Baer took the heavyweight world title from Carnera in a battle that saw the Italian hit the canvas no less than ten times. The referee finally brought the contest to a halt in the eleventh round.

Above: Carnera hits the deck and looks up to see Baer prowling around for the kill. The Italian got to know the canvas well and Baer became champion in the eleventh round.

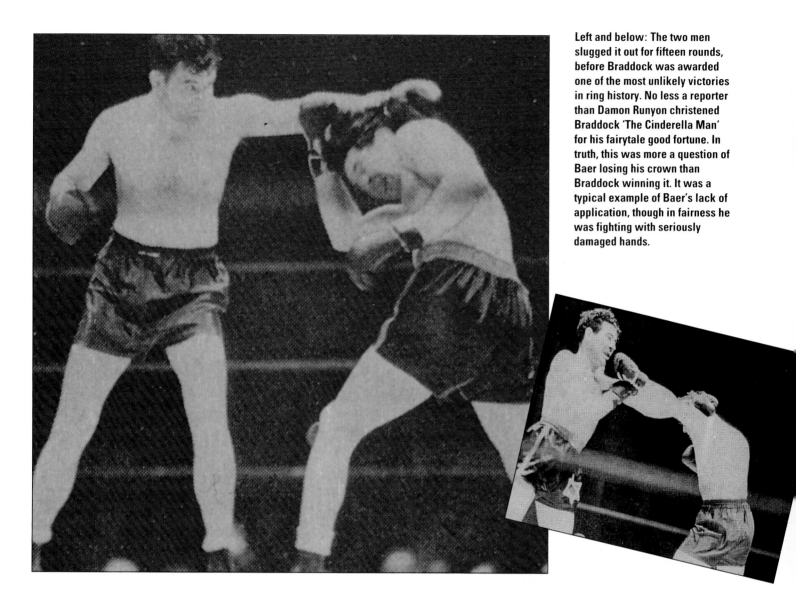

Left and below: The two men slugged it out for fifteen rounds, before Braddock was awarded one of the most unlikely victories in ring history. No less a reporter than Damon Runyon christened Braddock 'The Cinderella Man' for his fairytale good fortune. In truth, this was more a question of Baer losing his crown than Braddock winning it. It was a typical example of Baer's lack of application, though in fairness he was fighting with seriously damaged hands.

MAX BAER V JIMMY BRADDOCK

June 13 1935
Long Island

Baer lost the world heavyweight title to the unfancied Braddock in his first defence. The fifteen-to-one outsider, who had been given virtually no chance of winning, became known as the 'Cinderella Man' after his shock points victory.

Left: The winner was as surprised by the result as the crowd. A stupefied Braddock salutes his victory with a clenched fist. Baer later said that he had not taken the fight seriously enough.

MAX BAER V JOE LOUIS

September 24 1935
New York

Soon after losing his heavyweight title to Jimmy Braddock, Baer fought the up-and-coming Joe Louis. It was a one-sided contest that ended in the fourth round and it placed Louis in line for a world championship challenge.

Above and left: Baer was no match for the classy Louis (below) who started as favourite and was younger and fitter.

JOE LOUIS V MAX SCHMELING

June 19 1936
New York

Louis, a rising star, met the former world champion Schmeling in a non-title fight in Yankee Stadium. He had been undefeated in twenty-seven fights, but the experienced German had detected a weakness in the American's defence and succeeded in knocking him out in the twelfth round.

Above: Portraits of Louis and Schmeling at the time, and a scene from early in the fight, as both boxers probe for an attacking opportunity.

Right and far right: The wily Schmeling, a good tactician, had studied hard, and worked out Louis' weaknesses. He was able to trade on these in the twelfth by breaking through the 'Brown Bomber's' defence and sinking him to the canvas.

Above: Britain's Tommy Farr.

Left, below and bottom: Tommy Farr was born in Tonypandy, Wales, and his first career was as a coalminer. In an era when British heavyweights earned little respect in the USA, he beat Tommy Loughran, Bob Olin and Max Baer on his way to meet Louis. Still given no chance, he took Louis all the way, and the bruising bout, which is still talked about with awe in the Welsh valleys, won him great acclaim.

JOE LOUIS V TOMMY FARR

August 30 1937
New York

Louis became heavyweight champion on beating James J Braddock in 1937. His first defence was supposed to be an easy contest, but Farr put up a spirited effort and took the new champion the distance before losing on points.

Right: Ambers plummets to the canvas in the fifth round after a combination of punches from Armstrong. Luckily, or possibly unluckily, he was saved by the bell.

Above: A left jab from Armstrong has Ambers in trouble towards the end of the fight. Armstrong was able to keep going non-stop throughout the contest because he had an abnormally slow heartbeat.

HENRY ARMSTRONG V LOU AMBERS

August 17 1938
New York

With the featherweight and welterweight titles already in his trophy cabinet, Armstrong wanted a third and so took on Ambers for the lightweight world championship. The fight ended in a points victory for Armstrong, who consequently became the first, and last, person to hold three world titles simultaneously.

Right: Henry Armstrong becomes the first man to hold three titles at the same time. Far right: Armstrong undoubtedly qualifies as an all-time great.

JOE LOUIS V BILLY CONN

June 18 1941
New York

Right: During the early rounds, Conn showed that he was not afraid of the champion and launched fast attacks that forced Louis on to the defensive.

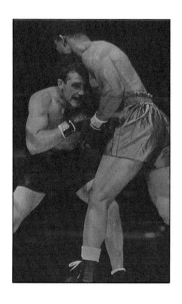

Above: As the fight wore on, Conn caught Louis in clinches and taunted the champion with verbal abuse.

Conn was the reigning light-heavyweight champion, and although the odds were against him, he was no 'Bum of the Month'. This challenger gave the heavyweight title holder a big surprise and nearly grabbed the championship for himself before being knocked out in the thirteenth round.

Left: Deciding enough was enough, Louis ended the fight in the thirteenth round with a series of punches that had Conn reeling.

Right: Beaten but unbowed, Conn manages a smile as he talks to reporters after the fight.

'SUGAR' RAY ROBINSON V JAKE LAMOTTA

February 23 1945
New York

Below: Jake LaMotta had come up the hard way: he later admitted that he was only allowed a championship fight because he agreed to throw a match for the gangsters who controlled the fight game in the 1940s – and that it cost him $20,000 on top of that. His world title fight against Cerdan was still four years ahead: many think that by the time he was allowed to challenge, his best years were past.

Above: The legendary 'Sugar' Ray Robinson. His first ever loss (after forty successive victories) was against LaMotta, on February 5 1943, and thereafter their rivalry became one of the greatest in ring history.

Jake LaMotta fought 'Sugar' Ray Robinson five times before he finally won the middleweight title in 1949. Robinson came out on top in four of the fights but each was a classic contest and the bout in 1945 was no exception. Robinson won the ten-round bout on points and went on to prove that he was still the superior boxer six years later when he beat LaMotta for the fifth time to wrest the middleweight crown from the 'Bronx Bull'.

Above: Robinson (right) catches LaMotta with a punishing left to the head on his way to a points decision.

TONY ZALE V ROCKY GRAZIANO

July 16 1947
Chicago

Zale and Graziano fought each other three times for the world middleweight title and this contest in 1947 was the only one in which Graziano emerged the victor. It was a tough, brawling battle and Zale later felt bitter that the referee had stopped the contest in the sixth round, claiming that he could have carried on and won.

Top left and top right: The two men who fought out a three-bout series in the 1940s that lives on in legend as one of the greatest ever: Tony Zale (left) and Rocky Graziano.

Above: A beautifully balanced and positioned Zale turns a left jab into a punch that stuns Graziano.

Left: Later, Zale, perhaps over-confident, let Graziano back into the fight. He always claimed that this scene, from the fifth round, was not nearly as bad as it looked, and that Graziano had pushed him into the ropes. The referee took a different view. In the sixth, the fight was stopped: again, Zale was outraged, feeling he could have gone on to win. To his eternal pride, Zale never went down.

GUS LESNEVICH V FREDDIE MILLS

May 14 1946
Harringay Arena, London

In Great Britain, the post-war boxing boom got under way with one of the light-heavyweight division's greatest fights. Promoter Jack Solomons matched the popular Freddie Mills with American Gus Lesnevich in a contest that would clear up the confusion as to who was the world champion. Lesnevich was recognized in the States; and in Britain, by virtue of his quick win over Len Harvey, Mills's claims had validity.

It looked as if it would never go three rounds once Lesnevich got into his stride – and he did so very quickly with some deadly precision punching. Mills was bounced off the ring floor for several long counts during the first two rounds and he barely made it to his corner. It looked all over but Freddie had guts and stamina. He came out for the third round and took the fight to the American. This assault continued through to round ten by which time Lesnevich's left eye was bunged up shut, his nose was bleeding and defeat looked imminent. It was at this stage that Mills became careless and was dropped heavily by a solid right. Lesnevich seized his opportunity and put Mills down

again. Referee Eugene Henderson called a halt with just a few seconds of the round left. A great fight was over.

It took two years for the two men to be rematched and this was, in contrast, a tame affair. Mills abandoned his usual style and boxed carefully to win on points. There was just one moment of excitement when Lesnevich was decked twice but he survived to go the full course. Mills held the title for two years before losing it to Joey Maxim. Lesnevich was also beaten by Maxim, and after an unsuccessful crack at Ezzard Charles's NBA heavyweight championship, he retired.

Above: Lesnevich taking one of two counts in the return contest at London's White City.

Left: Freddie Mills (left). His trainer, Nat Seller, and manager, Ted Broadribb, stand between the two fighters. To Lesnevich's left is his agent, Dave Edgar.

JOE LOUIS V TAMI MAURIELLO

September 18 1946
New York

The great Joe Louis's first post-war title defence against Billy Conn was a rather tame affair. Ring rust, the result of wartime inactivity, had slowed down both men. As a result, contenders were jostling to get a crack at the title. Tami Mauriello had put himself into contention by knocking out Britain's Bruce Woodcock. He knew that Louis was slower and more vulnerable than the vintage version, so decided to surprise Joe with an all out assault right from the first bell. He came straight out and tagged the champion with a solid right flush on the jaw. Louis staggered back to the ropes on unsteady legs and stayed there as Tami hesitated to capitalize on his advantage. Louis's instinct for survival then saved his title. When Tami came into range, Joe struck first. It was now the challenger's turn to be hurt, but there was no hesitating for Joe Louis. He finished his man off with a withering combination. Joe still had all his old power even if his reflexes had dimmed. One punch, as this illustration shows, lifted Mauriello clean off his feet. Louis was still the heavyweight champion of the world.

He defended his title twice more, then announced his retirement, but that decision didn't stick.

Below: Beating Tami Mauriello was Joe Louis's best post-war victory.

IKE WILLIAMS V BOB MONTGOMERY

August 4 1947
Philadelphia

Above: Williams scoring heavily with a left to Montgomery's head.

Right: Bob Montgomery, who was a very good champion until Williams relieved him of the title.

When these two men met in 1947, both had a claim to the world lightweight championship. Montgomery was recognized in New York because he had beaten Beau Jack in 1943, but the National Boxing Association disagreed and conferred their recognition on Sammy Angott when he beat Slugger White. Montgomery held on to his title but Angott lost his to Juan Zurita, who was in turn stopped in two rounds by Williams.

Ike had much more to motivate him than the chance to unify the title. He had been given a beating by the same Bob Montgomery early in his career and now had the added incentive of avenging that loss. It took him six torrid rounds to eliminate his old foe with an impressive display of power punching. Ike went on to become one of the greatest ever holders of the title. He made four defences before it became difficult to make the lightweight limit. He was drained when he lost his title to Jimmy Carter.

Cerdan (top right) dodges one of Zale's thrusting lefts. Zale concentrated on attacking Cerdan's body (above) in the hope that the Frenchman would lower his unusually high guard. This devastating right to Zale's head in the eighth round (right) marked the beginning of the end for the champion. Below: Marcel Cerdan.

TONY ZALE V MARCEL CERDAN

September 21 1948
Jersey City, New Jersey

Zale's reign as middleweight champion was brought to an end by Cerdan who became a French national hero. The Frenchman stopped the champion in the twelfth round.

Right: As if bowing in deference to the new champion, an exhausted Zale struggles to maintain an upright position after the fight has been halted.

Right: Joe 'Sandy' Saddler was born in Boston on June 25 1926, but raised in New York's Harlem district. On October 29 1948, in his ninety-fourth professional fight, he had taken the world featherweight title from Willie Pep in New York, and this was the first rematch in what was to become a famous series. He possessed a devastating punch, and it was this weapon that had caused the tremendous upset the year before, when he took the title against the odds with a fourth-round knockout.

Left: Willie Pep was born William Papaleo in Middletown, Connecticut, on September 19 1922, of Italian-American parents. He won the world featherweight title on November 20 1942 from Chalky Wright, and proceeded to hold the crown for nearly six years, before it was surprisingly taken from him by Saddler. Shocked into action, he was determined to get it back, and made no mistakes in this violent encounter.

SANDY SADDLER V WILLIE PEP

February 11 1949
New York

Saddler had defeated Pep in October 1948 to take the featherweight world title. In the return fight Pep had to resort to unorthodox tactics to regain his crown. He won the contest on points but lost two subsequent fights to Saddler in 1950 and 1951.

Below: Pep (left) breaks free from the constraints of the boxing handbook and launches a two-fisted attack on Saddler, leaving his head and body wide open. His target was the scar tissue around the champion's eyes.

'SUGAR' RAY ROBINSON V KID GAVILAN

July 11 1949
Philadelphia

This fight was Robinson's fourth defence of his welterweight world title. The Cuban challenger was supremely confident and, although he was soundly beaten on points, he did provide a few surprises for the champion and the outcome was in the balance until the very end.

Above: 'Kid' Gavilan was born Gerardo Gonzalez, in Camaguey, Cuba, on January 6 1926. This fight came early in his career, although he had been boxing since he was seventeen. His first fight in the USA was in 1946, but at this stage he was still seeking international recognition. His great years were still ahead of him, and he was to become world champion in 1952. He is above all remembered for a remarkable series of bouts against Billy Graham.

Above: Robinson (left) keeps a wary eye on the challenger, who nearly floored him in the eighth round with a flurry of hooks.

Right: Robinson won on a unanimous verdict that outraged all the Cubans who witnessed the fight.

EZZARD CHARLES V JOE LOUIS

September 27 1950
New York

Desperately needing money, Louis attempted a comeback in 1950 and challenged Charles for the world heavyweight title. The result was an easy points victory for Charles for by this time Louis was long past his best. It was not a popular win as Joe Louis was a national hero.

Right: Charles lands a left jab smack on Louis' face. The American public would have been happier if their favourite had remained in retirement. Even Charles was sorry when he beat his long-time hero.

Left: This was the end of an era. Ezzard Charles, together with Joe Walcott and Marciano, can be viewed as the first of the modern champions.

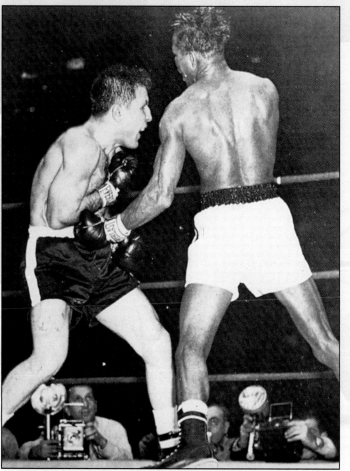

'SUGAR' RAY ROBINSON V JAKE LAMOTTA

February 14 1951
Chicago

Robinson won the middleweight world title for the first time by stopping LaMotta in the thirteenth round. This was the sixth time the two boxers had met: previous results were Robinson, four; LaMotta, one.

Left: The pain can be seen on LaMotta's face as he receives a savage blow in the midriff from Robinson. The referee stepped in to end the contest in the thirteenth round, awarding a knockout. Robinson's tactics had been to wear out the champion (albeit LaMotta was a year younger), and he effectively boxed 'The Bronx Bull' to a standstill. This fight brought to an end one of the greatest rivalries seen in the ring – their meetings were as follows: October 2 1942, Robinson wins on points in ten rounds; February 5 1943, LaMotta wins on points in ten rounds (this was the only defeat Robinson experienced in his first 133 professional fights); February 26 1943, Robinson wins on points in ten rounds; February 23 1945, Robinson wins on points in ten rounds; September 26 1945, Robinson wins on points in twelve rounds (split decision); final fight, as here.

'SUGAR' RAY ROBINSON V RANDOLPH TURPIN

July 10 1951
London

Turpin became the toast of England when he beat Robinson on points to relieve the champion of his recently won middleweight title. The Englishman only held the title until September of the same year, however, when Robinson stopped him in ten rounds to regain the crown.

Right: Turpin lunges with a left, and his aggression has the champion looking awkwardly unbalanced. Later in the fight, suddenly realising that Turpin had had the best of the early rounds and was ahead, Robinson started to attack and show better form, but he had left it too late, and the Englishman held on to win on points. Top: Robinson won the return match by stopping Turpin in the tenth round in September 1951.

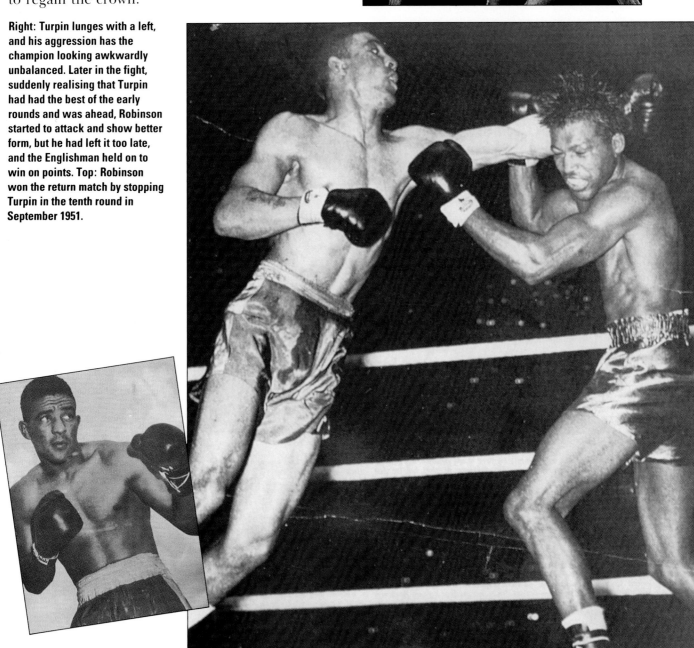

Above: England's Randolph Turpin.

EZZARD CHARLES V 'JERSEY' JOE WALCOTT

July 18 1951
Pittsburgh

Charles won the vacant world title over Walcott in 1949 on a points decision. In this second return fight, Walcott emerged as the better man and knocked the champion out in the seventh round. In a fourth meeting the following year, Walcott again proved his supremacy.

Top: Walcott had been given no chance in this fight, but they forgot to tell him that. This right was the beginning of the end for Charles, who moments later was finished completely by a powerhouse left hook. This was an emotional triumph for Walcott: he had lost four previous world title challenges – two to Louis, and two to Charles – but came good at thirty-seven to fulfil his dream.

Above: Charles is unable to stand up as referee Buck McTiernan kneels on the canvas to give the final count.

KID GAVILAN V BILLY GRAHAM

August 29 1951
New York

In one of the most controversial fights on record, Gavilan retained his welterweight title in a split points decision. Many who saw the fight, reckoned that Graham had done enough to win.

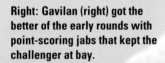

Right: Gavilan (right) got the better of the early rounds with point-scoring jabs that kept the challenger at bay.

Far left: Billy Graham was born of Irish-American parents in New York City on September 9 1922. He never became world champion, but was a great fighter whose main claim to fame was the series of contests against Gavilan (below). Unfortunately for him, Graham lost all four fights. This 1951 fight was originally intended to be for the US championship only, but at its close, Gavilan was controversially awarded the world crown despite the claims of European champion, Frenchman Charley Humez.

Left: In the closing rounds, Graham went on an all-out attack that very nearly won him the championship and convinced many spectators that he had edged a victory.

SANDY SADDLER V WILLIE PEP

September 26 1951
New York

Saddler and Pep met each other four times for the featherweight world title, with Saddler coming out on top in three of the contests. In this, their fourth fight, Pep retired from the contest during the ninth round, claiming that Saddler had fought dirty.

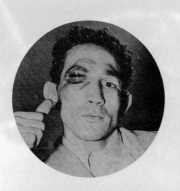

Above: Pep shows off his eye after the fight, with the obvious implication that the injury was caused by his opponent's head rather than his glove.

Right: Pep sinks to his knees in the second round after being stung by a combination of blows.

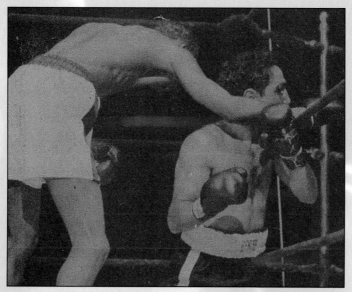

Below: This scene is from the third fight in the Saddler v Pep series, which took place at Yankee Stadium on September 8 1950. Stung by his defeat in the second encounter, Saddler came out strongly, and had Pep on the floor, and nearly through the ropes, in the third round. The result, a knockout win for Saddler in eight rounds, set up the keenly anticipated 1951 fight, which was to be their last meeting.

Left: Still early in the fight, and Pep (right) has Saddler bent double as he attacks his body. Things deteriorated after this, with less and less boxing taking place as the fight progressed. It was replaced by butting, gouging, tripping, and wrestling, and became a disgraceful brawl – one of the dirtiest contests in history. Pep was banned for life after the fight, and Saddler was suspended: Pep's ban was later lifted.

JAKE LAMOTTA V
LAURENT DAUTHILLE

September 13 1950
Detroit

Above: Dauthille is down and out against LaMotta.

Right: Dauthille (right) was in control for most of the fight.

With twenty seconds remaining of the middleweight championship fight between Jake LaMotta and France's Laurent Dauthille, ringsiders were getting ready to greet a new champion. The challenger held an unassailable points lead over the strangely sluggish LaMotta. Suddenly, Jake unleashed a right that shook his adversary. He followed up immediately with a barrage of savage punches that left Dauthille against the ropes, unable to rise. It had been a remarkably close call. Only thirteen seconds of the fight remained as the final ten count ended. There was no second chance for the Frenchman. He slipped into obscurity and died in poverty when still in his fifties.

JOEY MAXIM V
'SUGAR' RAY ROBINSON

June 23 1952
New York

Robinson, who had cleaned up the challengers for his middleweight title, stepped up a division to compete for light-heavyweight champion Joey Maxim's crown. It was an exceptionally hot evening and, for the only time in his career, Robinson failed to pace himself. He outboxed the champion and ran up a clear lead on points. In the tenth round the enervating heat of the Yankee Stadium forced the referee to be replaced but Robinson fought on at a fast clip. By the twelfth round Maxim's weight advantage, the pace and the cauldron-like temperature had slowed down Robinson. Maxim began to pile on the pressure, and in the next round Robinson missed with an uncharacteristically wild right swing and fell face forwards. He took a long time to rise on wobbly legs. Dehydration made him as limp as a rag doll and he needed assistance to get to his corner when the bell ended the round. He didn't come out for the fourteenth round. His dream of becoming a title-holder in three divisions was over.

Right: Joey Maxim (left) and 'Sugar' Ray Robinson.

Below: Robinson lands a punch to the body.

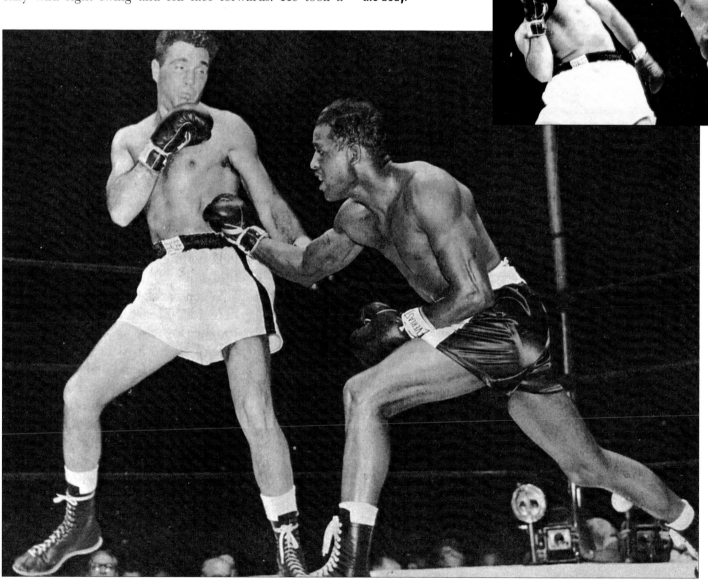

Right: Marciano pounded Louis to a humiliating defeat. The fight was stopped by the referee, Ruby Goldstein, in the eighth round.

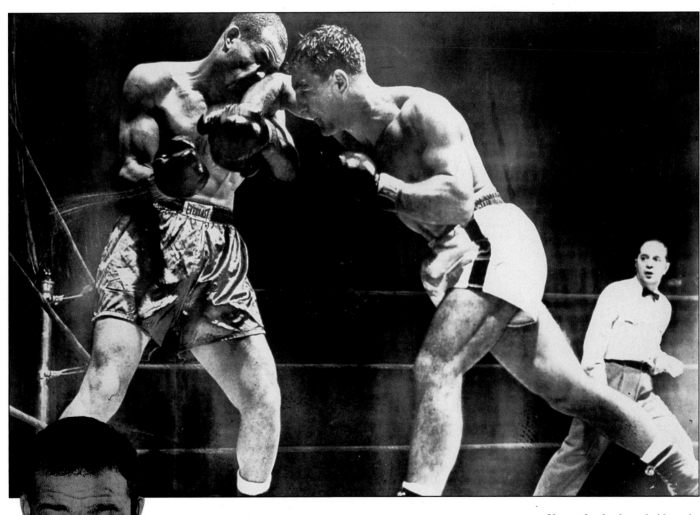

JOE LOUIS V ROCKY MARCIANO

October 26 1951
New York

In a comeback attempt to regain the world heavyweight title, Louis met Marciano on the understanding that the winner would go on to meet Walcott for the championship. Louis was by this time only half the great boxer he had once been and was savaged by Marciano throughout the fight.

Above: Joe Louis probably took more punishment in these comeback fights than he did through the whole of his main career. Like many great modern fighters, he came out of retirement for the wrong reasons, and to some extent tarnished his reputation. He should be remembered in his prime (far left).

'JERSEY' JOE WALCOTT V ROCKY MARCIANO

September 23 1952
Philadelphia

Marciano knocked out Walcott in the thirteenth round but he did not have it all his own way: until that point the defending champion was ahead on points. Walcott also had the satisfaction of decking Marciano in the first round but it was not quite enough and he took a terrible beating towards the end of the fight. In a return fight in May the following year, Walcott was a truly beaten man and lasted just one round.

Top: Walcott about to receive a massive blow from the all-powerful Marciano. However the defending champion was ahead until the fateful thirteenth.

Below: A typical shot from a Marciano fight: it is difficult to recognize Walcott through the pain.

ROCKY MARCIANO V EZZARD CHARLES

June 17 1954
New York

Marciano started as hot favourite to retain his title, and no-one expected Charles to give him much of a fight. The courageous former champion, did, however, stay the distance and he severely hurt the champion before losing on points. In the return match in June the same year, Charles succumbed in eight rounds.

Top: Marciano was backed to win at more than 3–1: he came in to the fight with forty-five straight victories under his belt, and was looking invincible. But Charles, drawing deep into his experience and courage, stood up to Marciano throughout, and ended with a points loss that, given Marciano's form, was perhaps the finest result of his career.

Above: Charles clubs Marciano with a right but the durable 'Brockton Blockbuster' was able to take punishment as well as dish it out.

Right: With a cut eye and a bloodied nose of his own, Marciano leans into Charles with a right. At the end, both of the challenger's eyes were closed and his face was badly swollen and bruised.

ROCKY MARCIANO V ARCHIE MOORE

September 21 1955
New York

Marciano retired after this fight, an unbeaten champion with a record forty-nine professional victories to his credit. Moore was knocked out in the ninth round.

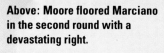

Above: The indefatigable Archie Moore. This fight only came about because of Moore's publicity campaign, but once it was set it was a winner. Moore was on a twenty-one fight winning streak, and although few truly believed that the light-heavyweight champion could beat Marciano, everyone wanted to see for themselves. The fight turned into the biggest boxing payday since Dempsey v Tunney.

Above: Moore floored Marciano in the second round with a devastating right.

Left: Referee Kessler helped Marciano to survive by forgetting that the mandatory standing count had been waived for this fight. When Marciano rose groggily to his feet after the second-round knock-down, the extra seconds Kessler gave him kept Moore at bay just long enough to allow Marciano to get his defences set. From then on Marciano piled on the pressure, finally knocking out Moore for good in the ninth. **Far left:** Marciano retired after this fight, a wealthy and happy man.

'SUGAR' RAY ROBINSON V RALPH 'TIGER' JONES

January 19 1955
New York

After his abortive attempt to win the world light-heavyweight title in 1952, Sugar Ray Robinson announced his retirement from the ring. This decision lasted three years, and during that period he saw many of his business ventures fail. There was one solution to these mounting debts – a return to the ring – and in January 1955 Robinson got a solid start by stopping tough Joe Rindone in the sixth round. Robinson's skills were still rusty and his management did not want him to take on the iron of the division for a while, so they sought a 'safe' opponent. When the name of Ralph 'Tiger' Jones was mentioned they accepted without hesitation. Jones had lost his last five fights, one of them being to the low-rated Frenchman, Jacques Royer-Crecy. He was durable and was expected to give Robinson a full ten round workout. On that assumption, Robinson's mentors were correct. What they had overlooked was that the Tiger was an experienced journeyman who had mixed with good company, and with the unlikelihood of his ever getting into title contention, he had everything to gain and nothing

to lose. Jones knew how to exploit Robinson's three years of inactivity. He fought at a pace, matching his man blow for blow, and turned up the pressure over the last few rounds. At the finish Jones was a narrow but clear winner. Such is the nature of boxing that Jones lost three of his next seven fights and Robinson had regained his old title before the year was out. Ray never asked for a return. The blot on his record stayed put while the great fights with Gene Fullmer and Carmen Basilio were yet to come.

Above: Robinson is short with a right to the body.

Below: Jones (left) watches for an opening as Robinson misses.

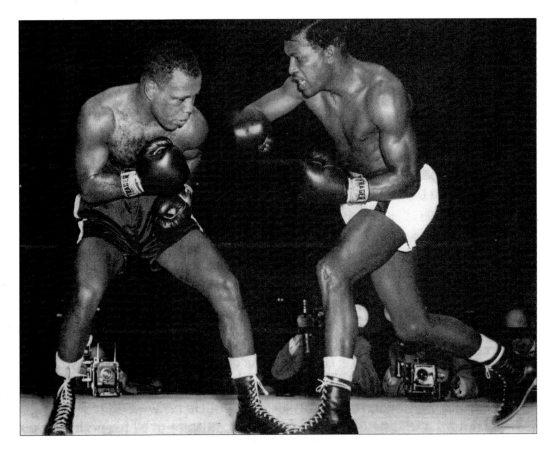

CARMEN BASILIO V TONY DEMARCO

June 10 1955 Syracuse
November 30 1955 Boston

Seldom do return fights match the intensity of the original encounters. A notable exception to that maxim were the two clashes between Carmen Basilio and hard-punching Tony DeMarco. The world welterweight title was up for grabs both times and both fights followed the same pattern of fistic mayhem. Basilio, a tough scrapper with a powerful left hook as his best punch, had never been off his feet. Apart from his innate toughness, he was game to the core. DeMarco could box, but his strength lay in his heavy punching and in both fights he started fast and battered Basilio to the head and body. Most of Basilio's fights were hard and he absorbed everything that came his way. When the pace that DeMarco had set slackened, Carmen went up a gear and took over. Both fights ended in the twelfth round with DeMarco taking heavy punishment – heavy enough, in fact, to force the referee's intervention. Both men withstood heavy punishment without going down, but it was the sheer persistance of Basilio that eventually prevailed.

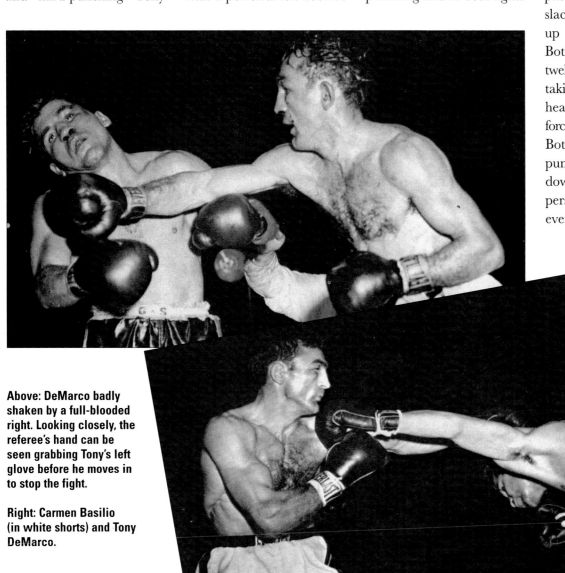

Above: DeMarco badly shaken by a full-blooded right. Looking closely, the referee's hand can be seen grabbing Tony's left glove before he moves in to stop the fight.

Right: Carmen Basilio (in white shorts) and Tony DeMarco.

GENE FULLMER V 'SUGAR' RAY ROBINSON

May 1 1957
Chicago

Robinson lost his middleweight title to Fullmer in January 1957 but regained it three months later in a return contest that lasted just five rounds. Fullmer later avenged this defeat, however, drawing a fight in 1960 and winning their fourth battle in 1961.

Above: Fullmer was so stunned by Robinson's flashing punches that he had to be told what had happened to him.

Right: In the fifth round Robinson was dominant and sent Fullmer to the canvas with a right-and-left combination.

'SUGAR' RAY ROBINSON V CARMEN BASILIO

March 25 1958
Chicago

Robinson had two classic fights against Basilio when the middleweight championship was at stake. He lost the first, in 1957, on a split decision but won the second, also on a split decision.

Left: Basilio ducks a vicious right uppercut from Robinson. The split decision went against Basilio, cutting his championship reign short.

Right: Carmen Basilio.

FLOYD PATTERSON V INGEMAR JOHANSSON

June 20 1960
New York

Having lost his heavyweight title to Johansson the year before, Patterson was determined to regain it. He dominated the rematch and knocked out Johansson in the fifth round. A year later he proved his point again by knocking the Swede out in six rounds.

Right and below: Johansson's principal claim to fame is his series against Patterson. He surprised him in the first fight, but Patterson got his mark for the others. Below, he can be seen hitting the canvas in the second fight: he stayed so still that Patterson thought he had killed him.

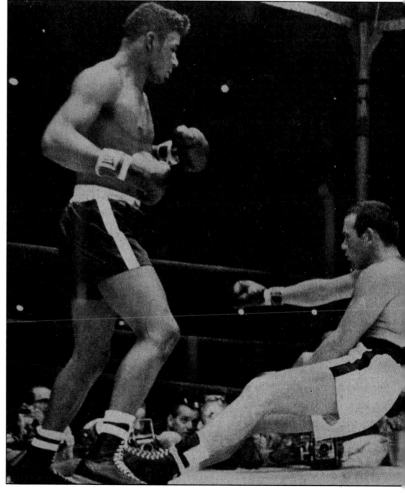

Top: In their first fight, on June 26 1959, Johansson knocked Patterson down seven times before the referee stepped in.

Above: In the third fight, in 1961, the Swede knocked Patterson down early, but the American came back to win in six rounds.

ARCHIE MOORE V
YVON DURELLE

December 10 1958
Montreal

This was one of the era's great fights, in which the old veteran Archie Moore survived a battering in the first round, boxed his way out of trouble and finished off Durelle in round eleven. It looked all over when Moore went down for the third time in the opening session. Moore was fast approaching his forty-fifth birthday and it seemed as if the years had caught up with him as his Canadian challenger set about him with blows that would have nailed any ordinary man to the canvas for good. But Moore was no ordinary man. His seconds worked on him like beavers when he got back to his corner. Somehow he got through the second round, and his strength gradually returned. Durelle was the younger man by sixteen years but it was he who couldn't stand the pace of the contest. By round ten Moore was very much on top and he dropped Durelle with a battery of punches only for the bell to ring as the count reached eight. Moore took no chances. He polished off his challenger within a minute of the next round. It had been a remarkable comeback from what seemed like certain defeat, and he was still light-heavyweight champion of the world.

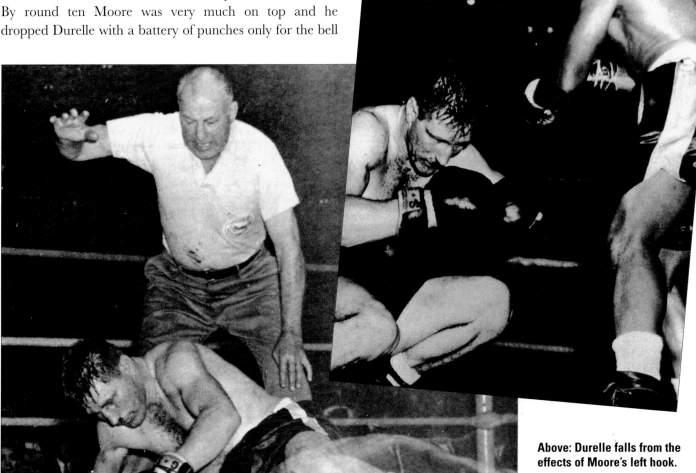

Above: Durelle falls from the effects of Moore's left hook.

Left: Referee Jack Sharkey counts out Durelle. The Canadian made a valiant effort to rise, but was still on the deck at the count of ten.

DAVEY MOORE V HOGAN 'KID' BASSEY

March 18 1959
Los Angeles

Nigeria's Hogan 'Kid' Bassey had come up the hard way. He got a shot at the world bantamweight title through a series of tough eliminating contests, and had to go to Paris to fight local hero Cherif Hamia to win the championship left vacant when Sandy Saddler retired. Bassey made sure of winning by stopping Hamia in round ten. He was a good champion and after he'd defended against Ricardo Moreno in Los Angeles, he stayed in the United States and defeated Carmelo Costa, Ernesto Parra and none other than the great Willie Pep who was then in the twilight of a long career.

A dangerous challenger loomed in the person of Davey Moore, who was known as 'The Springfield Rifle'. Moore was a brilliant boxer approaching his peak. He had Bassey badly bruised about the face by the tenth round. After three more rounds of punishment, the champion was fighting with impaired vision and had difficulty in seeing punches coming his way. Bassey, who had fought with a true champion's courage, hauled down his flag at the end of the thirteenth round. He knew that Moore was ahead and that further punishment awaited him. Like most men, he figured that he could win a return, but Moore was even better the next time. He won in similar style after eleven rounds. It was gallant Bassey's last fight. Over the next four years Moore retained his title against top challengers, then tragically was fatally injured when Sugar Ramos knocked him out. He was dropped near the ropes where his neck hit the bottom strand with lethal force.

Above: Bassey (right) is beginning to show facial injuries. Eventually, blood flowing from cuts impaired his vision to such an extent that the gallant Nigerian was forced to retire.

Right: Bassey is shown here in his prime. He left Nigeria in 1952 to campaign in Great Britain, but it took another six years before he got a shot at the world title.

GENE FULLMER V CARMEN BASILIO

June 29 1960
Salt Lake City

With a 1959 knockout victory over Basilio already to his credit, Fullmer was confident of another success at this encounter. The National Boxing Association's world middleweight title was at stake and Fullmer succeeded in retaining the title by knocking out Basilio in the twelfth round.

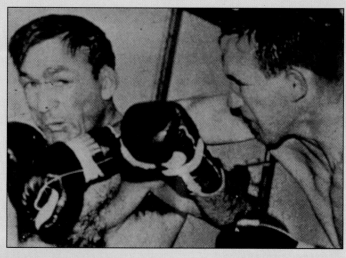

Above, left, and below: Fullmer was a rugged fighter: nobody admired him as a boxer, but plenty of opponents respected him. In this rematch with Basilio – no slouch himself when it came to aggression – he simply took over the fight and pummelled the ex-champion to defeat. Above: Fullmer's right scorches through Basilio's defence to score a hit. Left: the reigning champion is about to land the killer blow. It goes into Basilio's right side and knocks him flat – and very nearly out of the ring (below).

Left: Gene Fullmer was a Mormon fighter, born in West Jordan, Utah, on July 21 1931. He won the vacant NBA middleweight title by defeating Carmen Basilio in 1959, and held it until he was beaten by Dick Tiger in San Francisco on October 23 1962. After two unsuccessful return fights against Tiger he retired on July 23 1964.

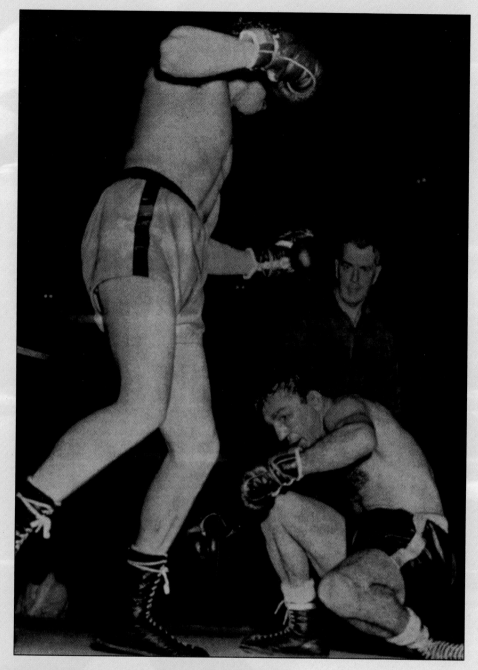

Left: Basilio takes to the canvas during the thirteenth round. He managed to climb to his feet, but lost the contest on points. This was the end of the line for the great man, who announced his retirement three days later. Basilio was born on April 2 1927 in Canastota, New York, and turned professional in 1948. His career spanned a golden age of middleweight and welterweight boxing, and during his fighting life he met such legends and fine fighters as Billy Graham (from whom he won the New York State welterweight title), 'Kid' Gavilan, Tony DeMarco (from whom he took the world welterweight crown), Johnny Saxton, 'Sugar' Ray Robinson, Gene Fullmer, and Paul Pender.

PAUL PENDER V CARMEN BASILIO

April 22 1961
Boston

Pender had taken the middleweight world title from 'Sugar' Ray Robinson in January 1960 and this was his third defence. He beat the former champion on points in a fifteen-round contest.

Left: With his head low, Basilio attacks the champion's midriff early in the fight.

Right and below: Benny Paret was born in Cuba on March 14 1937, and turned professional in 1955. He won the world welterweight title from Don Jordan in 1960, and held it until it was taken from him by Griffith on April 1 1961 in Miami. He regained it from Griffith, and then agreed to this rematch, which went terribly wrong when his head was knocked back against a ringpost in the twelfth.

BENNY PARET V EMILE GRIFFITH

March 24 1962
New York

In this tragic fight, Emile Griffith won the world welterweight title but the hapless Cuban defender died of injuries sustained when his head was battered against a steel ringpost in the twelfth round.

Right: Paret is eased onto a stretcher, oblivious of what is going on around him. He was taken to Roosevelt Hospital, but never recovered from his injuries, and died on April 3 1962. Griffith was distraught, especially when his attempts to visit Paret in hospital were interpreted by the media as publicity seeking: he was eventually able to put the memory behind him, and went on to win many championships. The fight had been shown live on American TV, and the effect on the image of professional boxing was understandably disastrous.

FLOYD PATTERSON V SONNY LISTON

September 25 1962

Chicago

Liston had to wait a long time to challenge Patterson for the world heavyweight title. He didn't waste a second when his chance came, and he flattened Patterson in the first round.

Right: After a nine-year wait for a shot at the title, Liston finished the champion in two minutes six seconds. Liston had an awesome reputation at this time: most professional boxers were frankly afraid of him. Patterson was brave enough to enforce the return fight clause in their contract, though most critics wondered why. In the event, on July 22 1963, he was again the loser: floored three times in the first, the knockout blow was timed at two minutes ten seconds.

Above: Liston (right) smacks Patterson on the jaw two minutes into the opening round. The challenger followed up with a left hook that put the champion flat on his back.

CASSIUS CLAY V HENRY COOPER

June 18 1963
London

The up-and-coming Cassius Clay, who later changed his name to Muhammad Ali, fought Cooper at Wembley Stadium in a non-title fight to decide who should be allowed a crack at the new heavyweight world champion, Sonny Liston. Cooper unleashed his fabled left hook at the end of the fourth round and put Clay on the canvas. All of Britain held its breath.

But Clay beat the count, and just as Cooper was about to finish off the groggy American, the bell rang. In the fifth round a cut above Cooper's left eye streamed blood and the fight was stopped. These seconds in the fourth when Clay was decked transformed Cooper, already a popular favourite, into a national hero.

Right: A legendary moment for British sport. If it hadn't been for the bell, and some between-the-rounds tactics by Clay's shrewd manager, Angelo Dundee, who knows what might have been? The break between the fourth and fifth round was timed at 90 seconds, as Dundee insisted on replacing a glove that Clay had split on his fall to the canvas. When he came out for the fifth, Clay was immediately back in action.

Above: With a badly cut left eye, Cooper launches a final attack at Clay in the fifth round; but it was not enough and the referee was obliged to call a halt.

Right: Clay (left), infinitely more agile than the ponderous Liston, leans back to avoid a slow punch from the champion. He was as wary as the rest of the professional fraternity of Liston's iron fists and enormous power, but knew that he could out-box and out-manoeuvre him. In the end, Liston, controversially, failed to get off of his stool for the seventh round. This dubious end to their encounter was as nothing to the controversy surrounding the rematch. In the least satisfactory heavyweight title fight of all time, Liston went down heavily after only a minute and a half of the first round – and very few people could see why. A short right-hander was thrown, but no punch was seen or filmed that could genuinely explain the despatch of a man of Liston's enormous strength, and rumour still abounds as to what really happened.

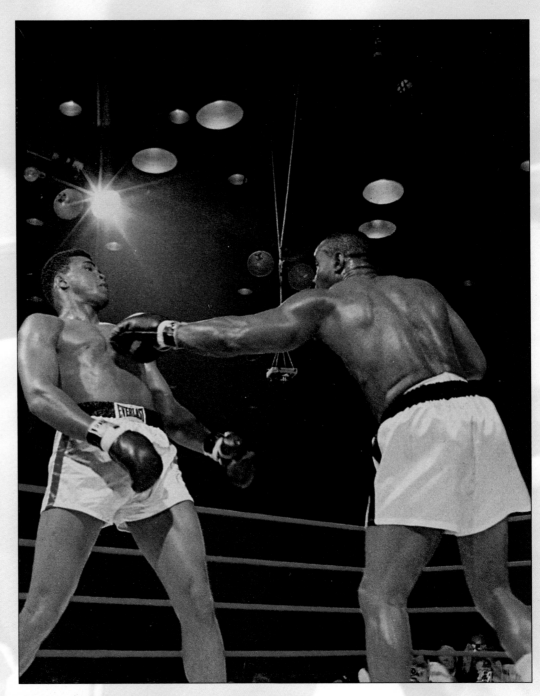

Below: Clay makes Liston's eyes squint with a left hook. By the fourth round, Clay was dominating the fight which ended when the defending champion refused to come out for the seventh round.

SONNY LISTON V CASSIUS CLAY

February 25 1964
Miami

The arrogant and brash Clay taunted Liston before, during and after this, their first fight for the world heavyweight championship. Liston was thought to be unbeatable but Clay survived the champion's initial onslaught and then took the initiative. Notoriously, Liston refused to come out of his corner at the start of the seventh round, and the greatest career in boxing history reached its first major peak.

NINO BENVENUTI V EMILE GRIFFITH

April 17 1967
New York

This was the Italian's first fight on American soil. He chose a difficult opponent amidst hostile surroundings but soon discovered that Americans support the underdog. The fans were to cheer even louder after his fine points victory in which the world middleweight championship changed hands. Benvenuti lost the return but won the rubber meeting. All three fights were classics in an era of some talented middleweight fighters.

Left: Griffith (left) scoring to Benvenuti's jaw.

Below: This is the second fight, won by Griffith, but Benvenuti got his revenge in their third meeting.

VINCENTE SALDIVAR V HOWARD WINSTONE

June 15 1967
Cardiff, Wales

All three of the Saldivar v Winstone fights were classics but the most controversial was the second. Set in Cardiff on a warm June night in 1967, this was, perhaps, Winstone's finest hour. All the skills acquired against the best of Europe's featherweights were put to use against the talented champion from Mexico. At the end of fifteen exciting rounds it looked as if the Welsh had a new champion in their midst but Saldivar had just scraped home due to his harder punching. All three of their fights were fought sportingly and cleanly. The two men became firm friends, and when Saldivar retired Winstone won the vacant title by stopping Mitsoneri Seki in nine rounds.

Above right: Winstone missing with a right.

Right: Saldivar sportingly raising Winstone's arm in acknowledgement of his brilliant boxing.

BOB FOSTER V DICK TIGER

May 24 1968
New York

Above: Tiger taking the count. This marked the start of Foster's reign. He became one of the great light-heavyweight title holders.

Right: Dick Tiger, who left his native Nigeria to perform in England.

This is the fight in which Dick Tiger went to the well once too often. He was a natural middleweight, and a good one, who settled in America and beat the best men in his division before winning the world title from Gene Fullmer. After losing this title to Emile Griffith, Dick set his sights on the light-heavyweight championship. He won this from the tough Jose Torres in his next fight. Dick was a tough scrapper and had never been knocked out, nor had he ever picked his opponent. Tiger fought them all, and did not hesitate to put his title on the line against hardpunching Bob Foster who was 6 feet 3 inches tall.

Tiger had difficulty in getting past Foster's long left and had to take a few heavy digs to get to the taller man's body. In the fourth round, he was working his way into an inside position when Foster caught him with a left hook that was perfectly timed. Tiger went down on his back and although he struggled to rise, he was too far gone to beat the count. It was the only time in his entire career that he'd failed to do so. This fight heralded the rise of Foster who would become one of the great light-heavyweight champions.

NINO BENVENUTI V CARLOS MONZON

November 7 1970
Rome

Monzon was almost unheard of outside his native Argentina when he first fought Benvenuti for the middleweight world championship. Yet against the odds, and in a staggering performance, he knocked the Italian out in the twelfth round.

Right: The great Carlos Monzon stands like a colossus over a stricken Nino Benvenuti at the end of their world middleweight title fight. Born in Santa Fe, Argentina, on August 7 1942, Monzon became one of the finest boxers ever to emerge from South America. He travelled to Europe in 1970 for the Benvenuti fight with a phenomenal record of eighty-two wins and only three losses in his homeland: yet most critics, presuming his wins had been against sub-standard opposition, gave him no chance against the Italian. His prospects were seen as particularly difficult, as Benvenuti was fighting in front of a home crowd in the hotbed of Rome: they felt that a knockout was the only sure way to get a result, and doubted that Monzon could despatch the strong Italian. But Monzon did just that, and then confirmed his superiority in the return match a year later. His next defence was against Emile Griffith, whom he stopped in the fourteenth round, and he then proceeded to defend twelve times more over the next six years before retiring. After retirement, his life deteriorated, and he was jailed for murdering his wife. While on bail in 1995, he was killed in a car accident near Santa Fe. He was only 52.

MUHAMMAD ALI V JERRY QUARRY

September 10 1970
Atlanta

After his enforced retirement from the ring following government legal action over his refusal – on religious and moral grounds – to be drafted into the United States Army, Ali announced his comeback in no uncertain fashion with a three-round victory over Quarry.

Left: Pain distorts Quarry's face as Ali hits him with a right to the head. The world had been waiting to see how Ali would perform after his lay-off.

Below: Ali catches Quarry with a swinging right to the head. It opened a bad cut above Quarry's left eye that led to the fight being stopped.

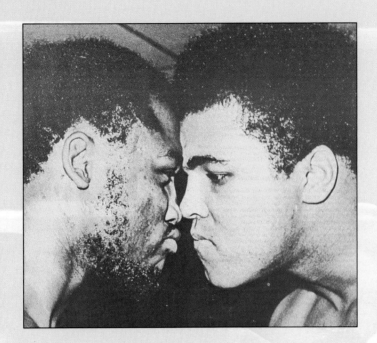

Right: This bout – the first of the modern 'superfights' – was hyped as an encounter between beauty and the beast. 'Ugly' Joe Frazier and 'pretty' Muhammad Ali obligingly posed for publicity shots – not surprisingly, as each of them was guaranteed around $5 million for the fight. Ali had forfeited the championship in 1967, and Frazier had unified the heavyweight succession by beating Buster Mathis for the WBC title in 1968, and Jimmy Ellis for the WBA belt in 1970. Ali, returning to the ring after a three-year absence, had fought his way up to challenge legitimately for the title he never lost.

JOE FRAZIER V MUHAMMAD ALI

March 8 1971
New York

In one of the greatest heavyweight title fights of all time, Joe Frazier saw off the challenge of the former champion with a points victory. Both men proved their strength, courage and stamina and both had to be hospitalized after the contest.

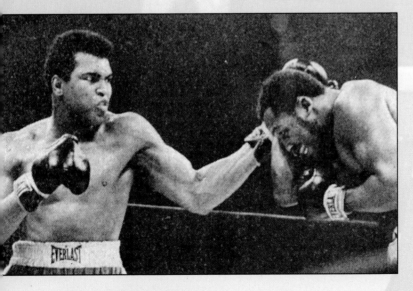

Above: The fight was by no means one-sided and the result was in doubt until the last round.

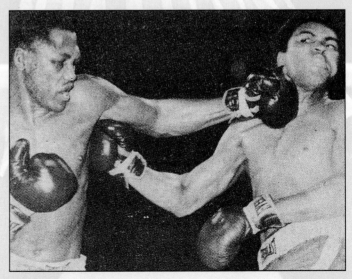

Above: Frazier thumps Ali's jaw with his favourite punch. It was the champion's left hook that did Ali the most damage.

Above: Ali's knees can no longer keep him up and he crumples to the canvas in the fifteenth round after Frazier has caught him with a hook. With a swollen jaw, Ali got up to finish the fight but lost the contest on points.

Right: The blow in the thirteenth round that Buchanan claimed cost him the title. It is clearly below the belt.

Above: Buchanan grimaces in agony after the illegal blow. The Scotsman claimed it was just one of several such punches, but the referee's decision is final, and he saw it differently.

KEN BUCHANAN V ROBERTO DURAN

June 26 1972
New York

Buchanan lost the WBA lightweight title to Duran after being hit by a foul blow in the thirteenth round. Although few would say that Duran was an undeserving champion, there was nevertheless an enormous amount of sympathy for the circumstances of Buchanan's loss.

Above: Buchanan leans backwards through the ropes a few seconds before the referee calls a halt.

JOE FRAZIER V GEORGE FOREMAN

January 22 1973
Kingston, Jamaica

Foreman had a reputation for being a knockout specialist when he met Frazier for the world heavyweight crown, but, even so, nobody dreamed he would take the title in the second round.

Left: In the opening round, Foreman forced Frazier on to one knee but the breather did the champion little good.

Above: Completely nonplussed, Frazier lurches against the ropes as Foreman looks on.

Left: Although Foreman was an Olympic champion, with a national reputation reinforced by thirty-seven consecutive professional victories, he was certainly not perceived as the man who would end 'Smoking Joe's' reign. But the younger man kept his head, boxed cleverly, and knocked Frazier down no less than three times in the first round. Frazier went down three more times in the second before the referee stopped the contest.

BOB FOSTER V CHRIS FINNEGAN

September 26 1972
London

By 1972, Bob Foster had established himself as one of the great light-heavyweight champions. With a shortage of challengers at home, he journeyed to London to put his title on the line against Chris Finnegan. Finnegan was a good boxer but lacked a soporific punch. The main thing in his favour was that he boxed from a southpaw stance and that was something that Foster was known to dislike.

Finnegan was a fighter who always had a go. After being dropped by a classic left hook early in the fight, he was still there at the start of the fourteenth round and was gamely matching Foster's attacks blow for blow. His only chance of winning was by the short route. Although he lacked the power to knock out a man of championship class, Finnegan chose to slug it out. When the effort of doing this left the Englishman exhausted, Foster was able to apply the finishing punches. Finnegan sat on the deck still conscious but too tired to rise. He had given it his all. Foster was never defeated for his title and announced his retirement after three more defences.

Right and top: Bob Foster (left) and Chris Finnegan.

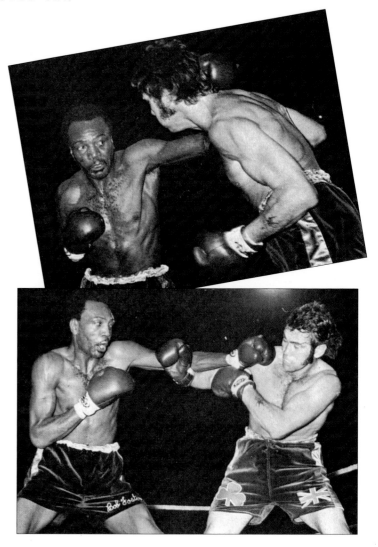

JOE FRAZIER V JOE BUGNER

July 2 1973
London

This was a fight that saw Bugner at his best. Frazier had just lost his world heavyweight title to George Foreman and was looking for a safe warm-up fight before attempting to regain the title. Bugner was too good for the European heavyweights but at world level could be judged solely on his losing fight against Muhammed Ali in Las Vegas. Ali, who had all the trouble he could handle against Frazier, won nearly every round against Bugner. Fighting an inspired battle, Bugner took the former champion to a close points decision at the end of which Frazier, with one eye completely closed, looked much the worst for wear. Bugner got off the floor to fight back. He took body blows that would have finished most other men, and fought back punch for punch. Eventually, both men fought Muhammad Ali for the big prize. Frazier had his last fight of any significance in 1976 but Bugner fought on for years and finally bowed out in 1999.

Left: Frazier (left) and Bugner in a grim struggle for supremacy.

ROMEO ANAYA V ARNOLD TAYLOR

November 3 1973
Johannesburg

South Africa's Arnold Taylor had a reputation for doing things the hard way but seldom has a man dug deeper into his resources than Taylor did back in 1973 when, figuratively speaking, he came back from the dead to take the world bantamweight title with one mighty, jawcrunching punch. Mexico's Romeo Anaya had a points lead going into the penultimate round. He had been down for eight in round five and had come back to drop Taylor for three long counts in the next. Taylor was in a bad way and his corner was ready to throw in the towel. Remarkably, the South African came back in round seven to repeatedly stagger the champion. It was Taylor's turn to hit the deck in round ten. Somehow he got up and, with a superhuman effort, tore into Anaya and had him groggy at the bell. The fight continued in its seesaw fashion for three more rounds in which both took heavy punishment. Taylor's right eye was closed; his cut lips and bruises on both cheeks gave him a frightful appearance. His final fling was one of the most dramatic in bantamweight history. He was the champion at last, but the punishing fight had taken its toll and he never rose to such lofty heights again.

Above: Taylor lands the punch that won him the world title.

Left: Arnold Taylor (right) stopped Romeo Anaya to become the new WBA bantamweight king.

MUHAMMAD ALI V JOE FRAZIER

January 28 1974
New York

In a non-title bout that was billed as 'Superfight II', the two former world heavyweight champions slugged out a gruelling twelve-round contest. Ali was this time declared the points winner on a unanimous decision.

Right: Both men fought their hearts out as both had a lot to prove. Some experts reckoned that Frazier's loss of fire power gave Ali an advantage.

Left: Though never billed as such, perhaps in deference to the reputations and dignity of the two participants, this fight was essentially an eliminator to see who would take on the increasingly fearsome Foreman for the heavyweight title. Of course there was enormous hype, and the two men received gigantic fees, but the event did not quite live up to its billing. It was, nevertheless, a hard-fought and genuine battle, with Ali taking the fight on a narrow, but unanimous, decision. Here he unleashes an uppercut, with Frazier ducking low. Ali was not his former, fleet-footed self, but he still had great stamina and courage.

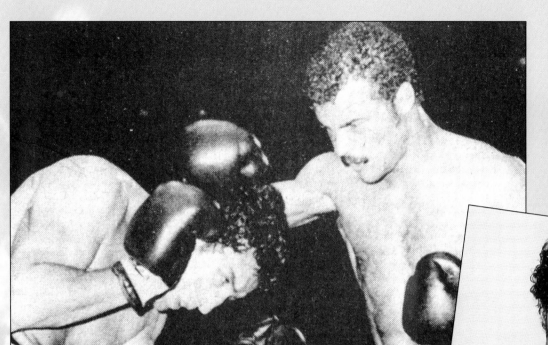

Left: Ahumada ducks under a right-cross from Conteh. Both men were fast movers as well as powerful strikers.

Below: Conteh had a win-at-all-costs style and attitude that did not earn sporting admiration, but brought great respect. This fight was the highlight of a career which did not go on to fulfil all of its promise.

JORGE AHUMADA V JOHN CONTEH

October 1 1974
London

In this contest Ahumada and Conteh fought for the WBC light-heavyweight title which had been stripped from Bob Foster. Although both men were cunning, strong boxers, Conteh came out the winner on points on this occasion.

Left: In the twelfth round the Argentinian's eye began to close, but he gamely fought on to the finish, only to be edged out on points.

Right: In the early rounds, Ali rested on the ropes and allowed Foreman to wear himself out. It was a dangerous tactic but, well executed, it paid off.

Below: Against all predictions, the referee intones the count as Foreman lies flat on his back in the eighth round, barely able to raise his head. Bottom: Foreman struggles in vain to get to his feet, and Ali becomes world champion for the second time.

GEORGE FOREMAN V MUHAMMAD ALI

October 30 1974
Kinshasa, Zaïre

Ali, the challenger for the world heavyweight title, called this fight the 'Rumble in the Jungle'. He boxed a clever fight, absorbing Foreman's attacks while resting on the ropes, and allowing the champion to exhaust himself by pummelling away at a carefully constructed defence. Then, in the eighth round, he cracked the tired champion on the chin and sent him plummeting to the canvas.

MUHAMMAD ALI V JOE FRAZIER

October 1 1975
Manila

'Superfight III' or the 'Thriller in Manila' lived up to all expectation and has been cited as one of the greatest heavyweight contests of the century. Both men were extremely brave and it was not until the twelfth round, when Frazier's left eye began to close, that either man had a worthwhile advantage. In the end Frazier retired in the fourteenth round, 'or else somebody would have got killed' as he put it.

Above: The punch that did the damage. Frazier's eye began to close up in the twelfth round and he began to take a great deal of punishment until the fight ended after the fourteenth round.

Right: For once a 'superfight' lived up to its billing. Don King set up his publicity machine, and involved the Phillipines government in supporting the fight at the Phillipine Coliseum, Manila. The world's press flew in, an audience of 28,000 turned up, 650 million TV viewers tuned in, and nobody will ever forget it. Far from sitting back, going through the motions, and collecting some of the highest earnings in ring history, the two men, each feeling they had something to prove to the world and each other, went at it as though it was their first title challenge. Whatever it was they wanted to prove, they succeeded: it was one of the most exciting and bruising bouts ever seen, and ended in the fourteenth, when the referee led a battered Frazier to his corner.

GEORGE FOREMAN V RON LYLE

January 24 1976
Las Vegas

This was the fight that proved to the critics that George Foreman had a fighting heart. Fifteen months earlier he had lost his heavyweight title to Muhammad Ali in Kinshasa, and there were many who said that he could have got up after Ali had put him down in the eighth round.

Lyle was a dangerous fighter with championship aspirations. After a couple of quiet rounds, he sprang to life and put George down for two long counts. Foreman came back to pound away until Lyle keeled over. He was finished, and Foreman had showed courage and a fighting heart to win in spectacular fashion. Big George was back!

Right: George Foreman (right) and Ron Lyle.

Below: Foreman down for the second time. He got up to win by a knockout.

LARRY HOLMES V
KEN NORTON

June 9 1978
Las Vegas

This was the fight in which Larry Holmes began his long reign as heavyweight champion of the world, but he had a difficult baptism. Going into the last round with Ken Norton, the points were evenly balanced. A last round rally got Holmes in front on two of the judges' scorecards. It was seven years before Holmes tasted defeat. As for Norton, he had only five more fights and retired after Gerry Cooney beat him in 1981.

Left: Larry Holmes held the heavyweight crown until 1985.

Below: Larry Holmes (in the white shorts) and Ken Norton.

Below: Ken Norton (left) defends himself from Larry Holmes.

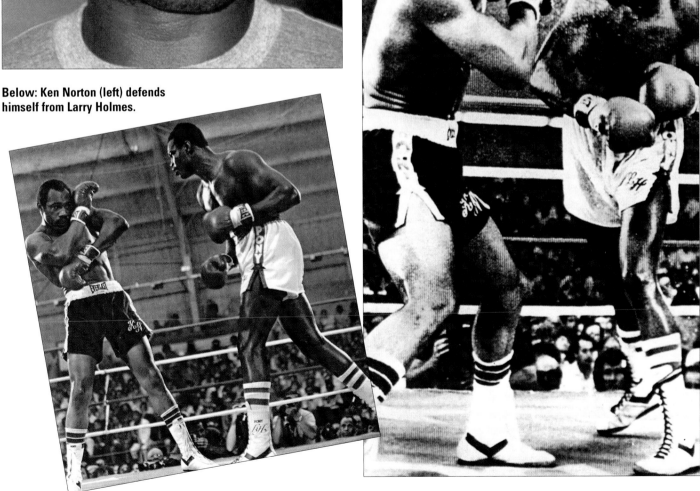

CARLOS MONZON V RODRIGO VALDEZ

June 26 1976
Monte Carlo

Monzon retired undefeated after fifteen world middle-weight title bouts. His last two fights were amongst his toughest – both were against Valdez. This was his first encounter with the Colombian and he won the contest on a points decision.

Right: Monzon dumps Valdez on to the canvas in the fourteenth round but the plucky Colombian got up to complete the scheduled fifteen.

Above: Trapped in a corner, Ali turns his back on Spinks who was much more aggressive than the ageing champion.

MUHAMMAD ALI V LEON SPINKS

February 15 1978
Las Vegas

Above: The decision is announced and Spinks shows his joy at gaining the championship by flinging his arms in the air.
Top: The young Spinks.

Ali lost his world heavyweight title for the second time in this fight. The younger man was stronger and more aggressive and eventually won on points. However the incredible Ali won a rematch in September the same year.

'SUGAR' RAY LEONARD V WILFRED BENITEZ

November 30 1979
Las Vegas

'Sugar' Ray Leonard relieved Benitez of the WBC welterweight title in this contest, but it was not an easy victory. Both fighters gave their all and it was not until the fifteenth round that a stoppage made Leonard the eventual winner.

Left: Benitez rocked Leonard with this left hook but the master technician came through to win in the end. It was a classic contest between two stylish boxers.

Above: The return fight proved to be one of the most controversial in recent history. On November 25 1980 Duran gave up his hard-won crown when he turned his back on Leonard (above) crying 'No mas' ('No more'). He was almost certainly frustrated by Leonard's style, but it took years for him to recover from the damage to his reputation.

'SUGAR' RAY LEONARD V ROBERTO DURAN

June 20 1980
Montreal

Roberto Duran took the WBC welterweight title from Leonard in this remarkable fight in which style was matched against slugging power. On the day, power won through, and Duran won on a points decision. Leonard, however, regained the title from the Panamanian five months later.

Above: Duran (left) succeeded in drawing the normally cagey Leonard into a toe-to-toe fist fight. His tactics proved successful.

MUHAMMAD ALI V LARRY HOLMES

October 2 1980
Las Vegas

This was Ali's penultimate fight and he was comprehensively out-boxed by the younger, fitter Holmes who was then the reigning WBC heavyweight champion. It was a sad defeat for the most famous sportsman in the world and even Holmes was sorry to see his hero beaten so easily. Ali quit at the end of the tenth round.

Right: This was a fight that should never have taken place, and, in retrospect, and seeing Ali today, it is obvious that the great ex-champion should never have been allowed to keep coming back into the ring. The fight was humiliatingly one-sided, and there was no credit to either boxer, nor to the managers, promoters, or the authority that sanctioned the bout. Ali tried one more fight, against Trevor Berbick, before retiring for good.

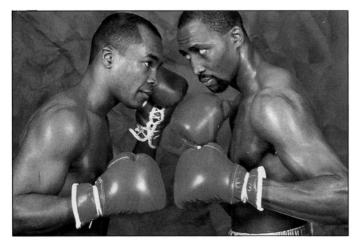

Above: The two boxers pose for a publicity picture before the fight (Hearns on right).

Right: In the fourteenth round Leonard launched an attack which had Hearns in so much trouble that the referee had to step in and call a halt.

'SUGAR' RAY LEONARD V THOMAS HEARNS

September 16 1981
Las Vegas

This fight was for the undisputed welterweight title of the world; Leonard held the WBC version of the title and Hearns the WBA version. It was a tough, evenly fought contest between two of the best boxers of the era. It ended when the referee stopped the contest in the fourteenth in Leonard's favour.

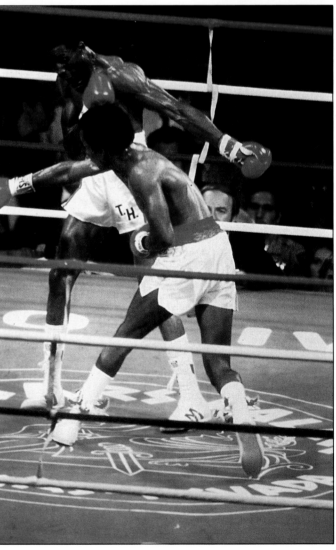

ROBERTO DURAN V THOMAS HEARNS

June 15 1984
Las Vegas

In this fight to unify the junior-middleweight world championship (Duran held the WBA version, Hearns the WBC version) Duran was overwhelmed and he was knocked cold and counted out in the second.

Right: Hearns (right) eyes his man warily, but it was Duran who was in for a shock. In the second round Hearns stepped in and knocked him out cold. Duran was in his seventeenth year as a professional boxer, and this was the first time that he had suffered such an indignity.

Below: This fight took place when Hearns was at his prime. His first title, the WBA welterweight, was won from Pipino Cuevas in 1980, but lost a year later to Leonard. Hearns had captured the WBC junior-middleweight world title from Wilfred Benitez in 1982, and this victory unified the division. He soon relinquished the title to move up to middleweight and challenge the likes of Marvin Hagler.

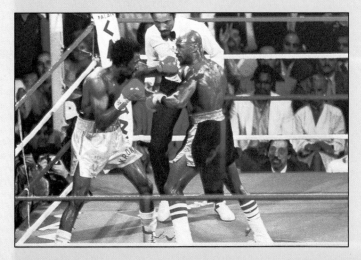

Right: Hagler (right) was the aggressor, continually moving forward to pressurize Hearns. The challenger had taken on a huge task: not only was he moving up in weight, but Hagler had by this time been middleweight champion for nearly five years, and had defended successfully ten times against the best in the division.

Above: The two champions pose before the bout wearing their championship belts.

Above: Hagler unleashes a mighty right that knocks Hearns groggy. Shortly after this punch in the third round the referee stopped the fight.

MARVIN HAGLER V THOMAS HEARNS

April 15 1985
Las Vegas

This contest was for the undisputed middleweight world championship. 'Hit Man' Hearns was the younger and taller boxer, but he was no match for the power of 'Marvelous' Marvin who dispatched the challenger in three rounds.

EUSEBIO PEDROZA V BARRY MCGUIGAN

June 8 1985
London

In front of a partisan crowd at London's Queen's Park Rangers football ground, the Irishman McGuigan took the WBA featherweight title from the veteran Panamanian. McGuigan won the contest on points.

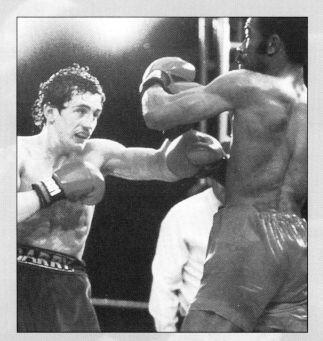

Left: McGuigan (left) appears tired towards the end of the fight, but the tenacious Irishman went on to win a famous points victory.

Above: Eusebio Pedroza, seen between rounds, was born in Panama City on March 2 1953. After turning professional in 1973 he quickly moved up through the ranks, winning the WBA world featherweight crown in April 1978 from Cecilio Lastra. He successfully defended the title nineteen times before meeting McGuigan in London, and came into the fight with an enormous reputation for durability.

Left: Pedroza (left) and McGuigan trade punches in the centre of the ring during their emotionally-charged contest.

BARRY MCGUIGAN V STEVE CRUZ

June 23 1986
Las Vegas

A last round rally, in which he dropped the champion twice, clinched the decision, and with it the WBA world featherweight championship, for Steve Cruz. The match was fought outdoors in 110 degrees heat and by the late stages McGuigan was badly dehydrated. That he survived the knockdowns to last the full course is a tribute to his courage. Cruz was champion for less than a year. He lost his title to Antonio Esparragoza in March 1987.

Below: Cruz (right) attacking with a right.

Right: McGuigan, one of the best Irish fighters.

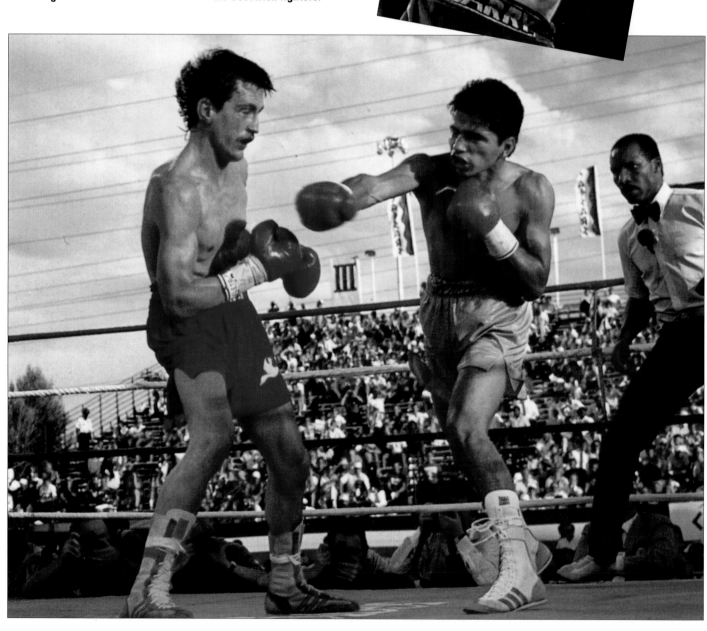

LLOYD HONEYGHAN V DON CURRY

September 27 1986
Atlantic City

In a huge upset, Lloyd Honeyghan stopped Don Curry in six rounds to win the undisputed world welter-weight championship. Honeyghan staggered Curry in the first round and the fight was still young when the defending champion had nose and eye injuries. Another cut, which was serious, appeared over Curry's left eye in the sixth. It was bad enough to force his cornermen into calling a halt. The legend of Curry's greatness had been badly dented.

Left: Lloyd Honeyghan being congratulated after his shock 1985 victory over champion Don Curry, previously regarded as invincible. Honeyghan stopped Curry in the sixth to become undisputed welterweight champion.

MIKE McCALLUM V DON CURRY

July 18 1987
Las Vegas

This was the fight in which Don Curry desperately wanted to prove to his critics that his loss to Lloyd Honeyghan was a fluke. He also had an added incentive. The man in the opposite corner was Mike McCallum and he had put his WBA light-middleweight title on the line. For four rounds the slick boxing Curry was in the lead, and it looked as if the title would be his when he staggered the champion with a tremendous one-two in the second round. McCallum admitted that he'd been hurt, but he was tough and he wanted to hang on to that title. He mounted an attack to Curry's body in the fifth round and then switched to the head. A lightning left hook then stretched the challenger out on his back. It was a spectacular knockout and one that diminished Curry's status as a contender. He was heading for greatness before the Honeyghan debacle and his past reputation got him a shot at Michael Nunn and later at Terry Norris, but he was beaten both times and also lost to Rene Jacquot in Grenoble. McCallum went on to be an outstanding champion in two weight divisions and was still fighting as he approached his fortieth birthday.

Right: Curry getting through with a right in the second round.

MIKE TYSON V
JAMES SMITH

March 7 1987
Las Vegas

In the first defence of his recently won heavyweight title, Tyson beat 'Bonecrusher' Smith on points in a twelve-round contest.

Below: The previous year Mike Tyson had become the youngest ever holder of the heavyweight crown, when, at the age of twenty years and five months, he crushed Trevor Berbick on November 22 1986.

Below: Tyson hits Smith with a right. 'Bonecrusher' failed to live up to his ring-name: he showed little aggression, and only lasted twelve rounds by alternately moving away from the champion and holding him.

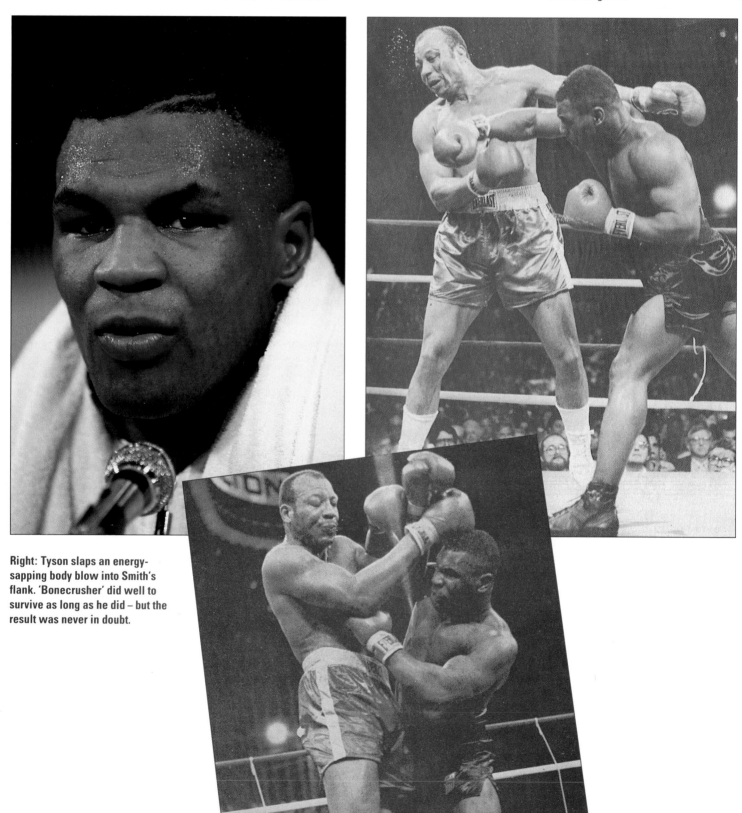

Right: Tyson slaps an energy-sapping body blow into Smith's flank. 'Bonecrusher' did well to survive as long as he did – but the result was never in doubt.

Left: Leonard (left) often boxed on the retreat, fully aware that if he tangled with Hagler he would get hurt.

Right: The more mobile Leonard (left) looks for an opening in Hagler's defensive guard.

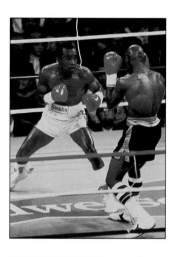

Right: Hagler was the more aggressive of the two, and his intention was to end the contest with a knockout. Leonard defended well on the move, all the while scoring valuable points.

Below: In the ninth round, Hagler drew Leonard into a brawl which boosted his chances of success, but in the end Leonard's skill, and the points he had already accumulated, won the day.

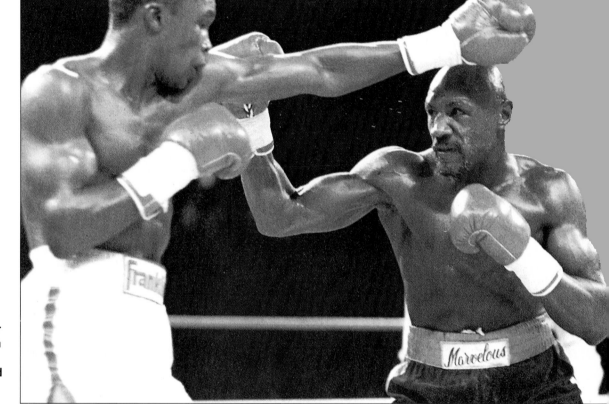

MARVIN HAGLER V 'SUGAR' RAY LEONARD

April 6 1987
Las Vegas

Leonard recorded an astonishing points victory over Hagler after a lay-off of three years during which he did not box a single contest. The fight was for the WBC version of the middleweight world championship and became the richest contest in boxing history. Leonard won on a controversial split decision – many observers reckoned that Hagler had done enough to win.

FIDEL BASSA V DAVE MCAULEY

April 25 1987
Belfast

In front of his home crowd in Northern Ireland, McAuley put in a magnificent effort in his attempt to wrest the WBA flyweight title from Bassa. He floored the Colombian several times before he himself was stopped in the thirteenth round. In a return match the following year, Bassa again came out on top.

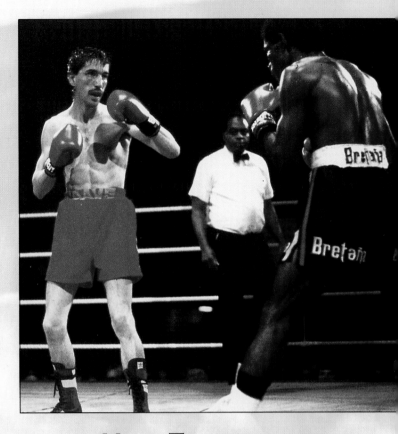

Right: McAuley (left) fought valiantly and skilfully, putting the champion on the canvas several times. However the champion retained his title when the referee saved the Irishman from taking a terrible hammering in the thirteenth.

MIKE TYSON V LARRY HOLMES

January 22 1988
Atlantic City

Holmes, the man who had beaten Muhammad Ali, was past his best and no match for the sheer strength and aggression of Tyson. The contest ended in the fourth round.

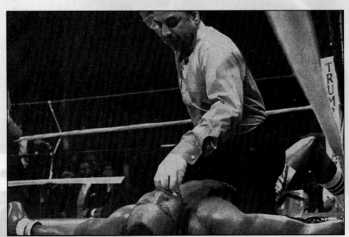

Left: The sluggish Holmes was completely overwhelmed by Tyson's non-stop assault.

Above: The referee takes the shield from Holmes' mouth as he lies flat on his back in the fourth round.

JORGE VACA V LLOYD HONEYGHAN

March 28 1988
London

Vaca had beaten Honeyghan on a technical decision the previous year to take away the Britisher's WBC welterweight title. Feeling that he had something to prove, Honeyghan came out strongly, and knocked the Mexican out in the third round.

Above: Fighting on his home turf, Honeyghan (left) went on the offensive and settled it quickly with a knockout.

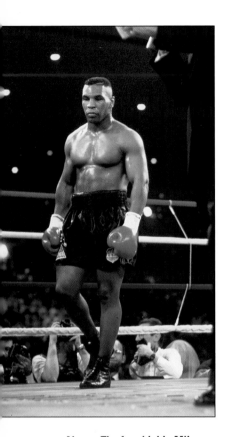

Above: The formidable Mike Tyson, victorious in the fifth round against the British challenger. This was Tyson's seventh defence: his other wins had been against 'Bonecrusher' Smith in March 1987; Pinklon Thomas in May 1987; Tony Tucker in August 1987; Larry Holmes in January 1988; Tony Tubbs in March 1988; and Michael Spinks in June 1988.

Above: Bruno started well, and at one point in the first round the champion was clearly shaken. But thereafter, Tyson found his form, and battered the Englishman to a fifth-round defeat.

MIKE TYSON V FRANK BRUNO

February 25 1989
Las Vegas

Bruno, England's favourite heavyweight, rocked Tyson in the first round which surprised everybody, not least the champion. However there was no major upset and Bruno had to be saved by the referee in the fifth round.

'SUGAR' RAY LEONARD V THOMAS HEARNS

June 12 1989
Las Vegas

This classic contest for the WBC super-middleweight title ended in a draw. Both men were past their best but they fought tenaciously and fortunes fluctuated both ways. It was the fight of the year.

Right: Hearns on the attack. Some experts reckoned that Leonard was lucky to get away with a draw as he was knocked to the canvas on two occasions.

DENNIS ANDRIES V JEFF HARDING

June 24 1989
Atlantic City

Andries lost his WBC light-heavyweight title to the Australian in this contest after dominating most of the fight. He was rescued by the referee from a punishing last ditch attack in the last round. Andries regained the title from Harding the following year with a knockout victory.

Right: Andries and Harding exchange jabs. The champion used his experience and technique to edge ahead in the early rounds, but, as he admitted afterwards, he knew little about the Australian (who was a late replacement for Donny Lalonde), and was shocked when Harding seemed to get stronger and stronger.

Above: This was Andries' first defence. He had picked up the vacant WBC title only months before by defeating Tony Willis on February 21 in Arizona.

Left: Jeff 'Hit Man' Harding resting between rounds. Together with Jeff Fenech, he is rated as the best boxer to emerge from Australia in decades. Virtually unknown outside his homeland, he got his shot at Andries as a late substitute, and was little fancied. His fantastic courage, and non-stop aggression, saw him home in an upset victory.

MIKE TYSON V JAMES DOUGLAS

February 11 1990
Tokyo

Tyson was thought to be invincible until 'Buster' Douglas knocked him cold in the tenth round. Douglas was not considered to be a major threat – or any threat at all – to the champion but he did the 'impossible'. He subsequently lost the world heavyweight title to Evander Holyfield in his first defence. His performance against Holyfield was so lame, and he had prepared for it so poorly, that most critics' view that his victory in the Tyson contest was a fluke and a flash-in-the-pan was convincingly confirmed.

There was some controversy over whether the referee gave a long count earlier in the fight but the final knockout decision was upheld. It later emerged that most of the confusion was, according to some sources, deliberately caused by Tyson's manager Don King, in an attempt to get his boxer's loss overturned. The conspiracy theory alleges that, to their shame, the authorities nearly went along with this, perhaps having it in mind that Tyson as champion was better for boxing than the unknown Douglas. Certainly there was chaos after the fight, and the result was not finally confirmed for several hours. In the end justice, and conscience, were served.

Right: Bowe lands a punishing right jab to the head of Evander Holyfield. The latter's attempt to trade punches with his bigger and stronger opponent proved ill-fated. He lasted the twelve rounds, having been knocked to the canvas in the eleventh, but by then the decision was in no doubt.

Right: A young man from the same Brownsville area of Brooklyn as Mike Tyson, Riddick Bowe's ability and determination look set to earn him an equally fabled position in the history of world boxing.

RIDDICK BOWE V EVANDER HOLYFIELD

November 13 1992 at Las Vegas
November 6 1993 at Las Vegas
November 4 1994 at Las Vegas

In three of the hardest-fought heavyweight fights of the nineties, Evander Holyfield and Riddick Bowe exchanged tenure of the championship. Holyfield said of their 1992 clash: 'Everything I did, he did better.' One year later, Holyfield boxed magnificently to win on points but the rubber match went to Bowe who rallied to stop his man.

CHRIS EUBANK V NIGEL BENN

November 18 1990
Birmingham

This was a grudge match between two British world-class middleweights, and the clash of styles produced one of the country's best-ever fights at that weight. It was Eubank's more accurate punching that prevailed against the aggression of Benn. In the ninth round Benn was having difficulty seeing. One of his eyes was bruised and nearly shut. Eubank, who was bleeding from the mouth, was still strong. The end came with Benn hacked against the ropes and wobbled badly. The referee let it go on for another few seconds, then called a halt. Benn's WBO middle-weight title, which he'd won from Doug DeWitt, passed into Eubank's hands.

Left: Chris Eubank recovered from this position to stop Nigel Benn in the ninth round.

CHRIS EUBANK V MICHAEL WATSON

September 21 1991
Tottenham

Controversy was never a stranger to Chris Eubank. His career encompassed twenty-six world title fights. Some he won spectacularly, some narrowly and some with ease, but one he would sooner forget was the return match that ended tragically with Michael Watson. They had met three months previously. Eubank had scraped home on points but Watson felt sure that he had done enough to get the verdict. This time, determined to leave no doubt as to who was the better man, Watson piled on the pressure from the start. Knowing that Eubank was not as effective fighting off his back foot as he was coming forward, he kept his foot on the accelerator and gave his old adversary few chances to get into his usual rhythm. The vacant WBO super-middleweight championship was at stake, and going into round eleven it looked as if Watson would become the new champion. With under half a minute left of the round, he became the first man to put Eubank down. Then it happened – he walked in to finish the job and ran into a terrific right uppercut that dropped him in a heap against the ropes. The bell rang before Eubank could capitalize but he finished the job only seconds into the last round. Celebrations were curtailed when it was apparent that

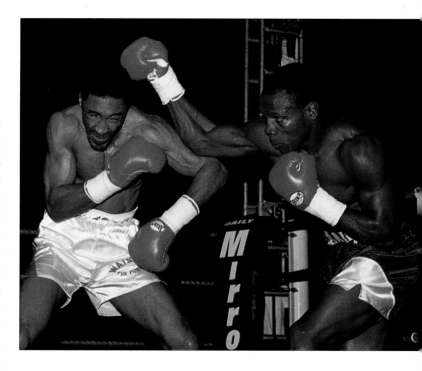

Above: Chris Eubank (right) beat Watson.

Watson was badly hurt. He was rushed to hospital and underwent brain surgery. His progress was slow at first and even nine years later he still had some way to go. Eubank boxed on, but the scars of that night remained and he often seemed reluctant to finish off men he had dominated with his clever brand of boxing.

AZUMAH NELSON V JEFF FENECH

March 1 1992
Melbourne

There were cries of "robbery" when Azumah Nelson kept his world title by boxing a draw with Aussie challenger Jeff Fenech in 1991. It was on open-air contest in Las Vegas and supported Mike Tyson's second win over Razor Ruddock. Fenech never stopped attacking, but many of his blows hit Nelson's arms whereas the quality work came from the Ghanian. Nelson, it was later rumoured, came off a sick bed to defend his title. Certainly, he was a far cry from his usual self and the alacrity with which he agreed to a return in Fenech's 'hometown' arena in Melbourne should have rung a few warning bells, but the Australian was an odds-on favourite in the betting.

If anything, Fenech boxed better the second time – boxed, that is, rather than fought, because the heavy punching came from the champion, who took control quickly and put Fenech down in the first and second rounds. Fenech gamely took the fight to the champion for another six rounds but was being picked off with some hard counters. Nelson finished it with a flourish in the eighth round. He sent Fenech sprawling with a right to the head and, at this stage, referee Arthur Mercante called a halt.

Below: Azumah Nelson (left) and Jeff Fenech both missing with straight lefts.

Right: Jeff Fenech.

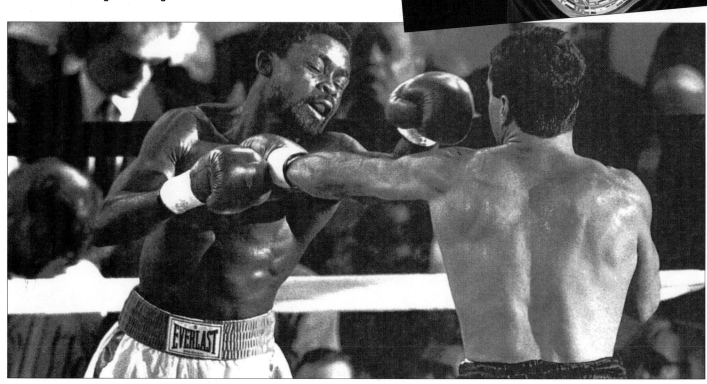

FRANKIE RANDALL V JULIO CESAR CHAVEZ

January 29 1994
Las Vegas

15–1 outsider Frankie Randall spoiled the hitherto unbeaten record of WBC light welterweight champion Julio Cesar Chavez by taking a 12 round points decision. To add insult to injury, Randall put Chavez down for a count of eight in the eleventh round.

Above: It was a thrilling and extremely closely-contested encounter, largely decided by the two points that referee Richard Steele ordered to be deducted from Chavez for low blows.

Right: Boxing's longest unbeaten record draws to an end, as Randall soaks up a little punishment and wears down the champion to a 12-round points defeat. Chavez lost his composure after the bout, and his post-fight behaviour and comments were felt by some to have tarnished a great career.

GEORGE FOREMAN V MICHAEL MOORER

November 5 1994

Las Vegas

Evergreen George Foreman became heavyweight champion for the second time when, at the advanced age of 45, he knocked out WBA and IBF title holder Michael Moorer in the tenth round.

Right: Moorer was born in the year of Foreman's first great triumph – the Olympic Gold Medal win of 1968. As the fight went on past the fifth and sixth rounds the assumption from fans and gamblers was that youth would tell – no-one realistically backed Foreman to last the pace.

Right: Foreman took punishment throughout the fight, then surprised everyone by going on to the attack. Most experts feel he would have lost the decision if the fight had gone the full twelve rounds – and maybe it was this feeling that spurred Foreman forward.

Left: Moorer always had a suspect chin, and Foreman's main hope was to find this target. As the crowd chanted his name – some forlornly – Big George finally put together a pinpoint combination in the tenth that hit the spot, flooring Moorer to grab the title.

ROY JONES V JAMES TONEY

November 18 1994
Las Vegas

One of the most eagerly awaited clashes in the super middleweight division took place when these two unbeaten men fought for Toney's IBF championship. Jones showed superb skills and dazzling speed to win clearly on points and to establish himself as one of the greatest fighters of his era.

Left: On the night, Jones was just too good and too quick for Toney. Toney later stated that he had problems with making the weight, and that he was suffering from flu. But in truth he was stylishly and convincingly beaten by one of the top boxers in the world.

Below: It was not all plain sailing, and Jones is seen here reeling from a Toney attack. But Toney lacked the consistency, and apparently the energy, to hold off the Jones juggernaut.

LENNOX LEWIS V OLIVER McCALL

September 24 1994
Wembley Arena

On paper, this looked like being a routine defence of his WBC heavyweight championship for Britain's Lennox Lewis. He'd already beaten off three previous challengers and was marking time until he could get Riddock Bowe in the opposite corner to unify the world championship. Bowe put too many obstacles in the way and his eagerly awaited clash with Lewis was destined to become one of the big fights that never happened.

Lewis liked to keep active, and when McCall's name was suggested as his next challenger, he agreed. The American had a rather spotty record with five defeats in twenty-nine fights, but he was a strong puncher and had a burning ambition to make the most of this chance to get into the big time.

Lewis had little difficulty in getting through with his long left jab but he was also sloppy with it, and McCall's cornermen soon saw the key to success as Lennox let his guard down.

In those opening three minutes, McCall had found out all he wanted about the strengths and weaknesses of the defending champion. The second round was less than a minute old when Lewis was beaten to the punch. He started a right to McCall's head but dropped his left hand far too low. It was the opening that the challenger wanted. He put everything behind a right to the jaw and the punch zeroed home. Lewis went on to his back and into the ranks of ex-title-holders. He got up but was too groggy to continue. The round was young and McCall would never have let him last another two minutes. This was the biggest fistic upset of the year, but instead of heralding the start of a new champion's reign it was the start of McCall's slide into oblivion. He drifted into the world of drugs, lost his title to Frank Bruno and failed miserably to repeat his previous form in a rematch with Lewis when he broke down during the fight and was reduced to tears. Lewis became undisputed champion five years later.

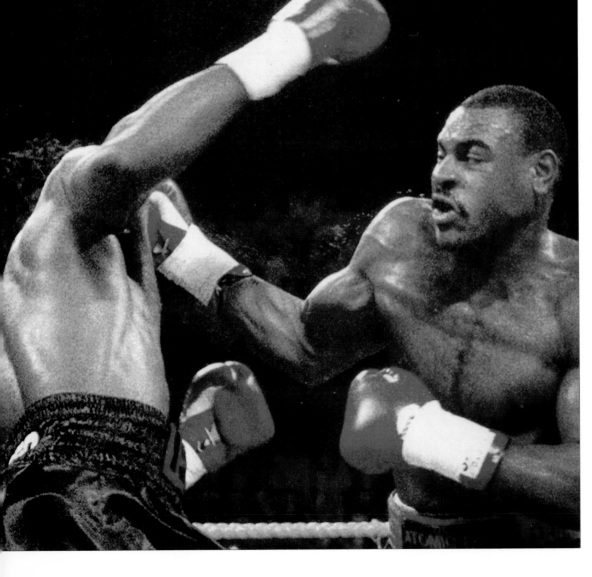

Left: Oliver McCall lands the right that beat Lennox Lewis.

AZUMAH NELSON V
GABE RUELAS

December 1 1995
California

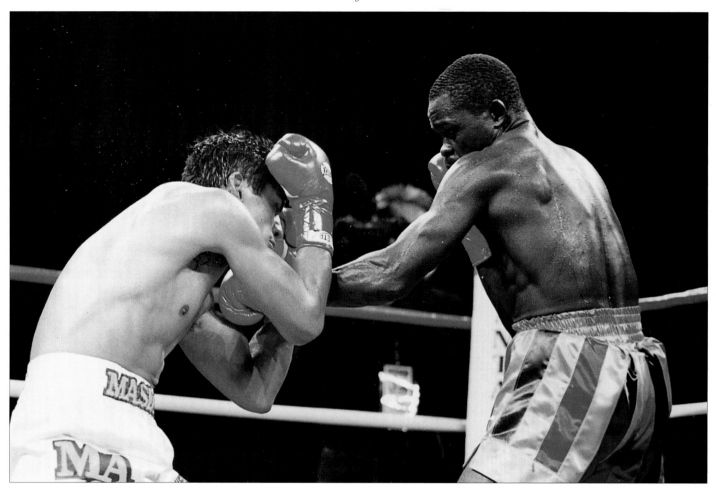

Above: Azumah Nelson just would not let Gabe Ruelas off the hook.

At age thirty-seven, an age when boxing critics considered that his best days were long gone, the great Azumah Nelson turned in a superb performance to regain the WBC super-featherweight title from a man who had given him a tough fight three years previously. Defending champion Gabe Ruelas from Mexico, a great favourite at the open-air Indian Springs Casino, had the crowd behind him, but Nelson was a man who'd made a career habit of stepping into his opponent's backyard to upset the odds.

Nelson had trained diligently and showed no signs of rust after a 19-month period of inactivity. He was ready for anything the champion threw at him. The crowd was behind Ruelas and a mighty din reverberated around the arena as he came out like an express train to take the fight to Nelson. The cheers were silenced when just over a minute into the fight Nelson slammed over a left-right combination that sent Ruelas down hard. Azumah showed great coolness at this stage. Instead of rushing in to finish the fight, he calmly picked his punches and hurt Ruelas to both the body and head. A left hook thrown just before the end of round two had the champion in trouble again.

With a minute to go of round four, and with Ruelas showing signs of distress, Nelson turned up the heat and pummelled the Mexican's body before flooring him with a salvo of left hooks. Gabe got the benefit of a long count that enabled him to somehow survive until the bell. Nelson is as good a finisher as any featherweight in boxing history. After a minute and twenty seconds of the fifth round, referee Marty Denkin jumped in to halt the slaughter. This was the fourth world title to grace Nelson's record and a fight that would confirm his place among the great champions of the modern era.

NIGEL BENN V GERALD MCCLELLAN

February 25 1995
London Docklands Arena

A stirring but brutal encounter at London Docklands Arena ended in near tragedy when Gerald McClellan collapsed after being counted out in the tenth round. Benn, defending his WBC super-middleweight title, barely survived a first round knockdown and then came from behind to outlast and outpunch a brave challenger who required brain surgery following the surprise ending.

Left: Something went seriously wrong for McClellan in the tenth round. Going in to it he looked fit and strong, then suddenly he was down, with many at the ringside left wondering why. Later debate questioned whether he had over-trained, over-fasted, or whether he had just taken a bad beating because he had under-estimated the strength and skill of his opponent. He took a slow road to recovery after post-fight surgery.

Right: It was a much different story earlier, as McClellan knocked Benn down in both the first and eighth rounds. Benn showed incredible resilience and determination in coming back to a victory which, though clouded by McClellan's predicament, was nevertheless well earned.

EVANDER HOLYFIELD V MIKE TYSON

MGM Grand Casino, Las Vegas, November 9 1996

25–1 underdog outgames, outboxes and outpunches the feared Mike Tyson in eleven bitterly fought rounds to win the WBA title in one of the heavyweight division's greatest fights.

Below: Holyfield shows an iron resolve against the mighty blows that have crushed other heavyweights.

Left: Tyson totters on his feet at the end of the 10th round – 37 seconds later it was all over.

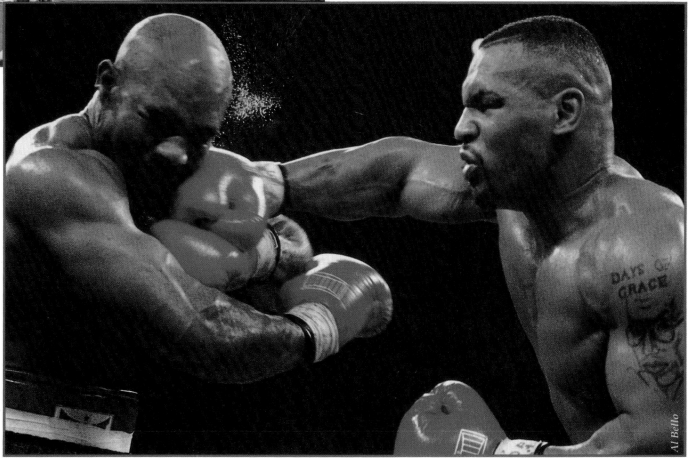

Al Bello

LENNOX LEWIS V ANDREW GOLOTA

October 4 1997
Atlantic City

In 95 seconds Lennox Lewis silenced his critics as he destroyed a very dangerous challenger in Andrew Golota. This was going to be a fight that would test Lewis – one that would make him dig deep to win. Golota, from Poland, had finished the career of Riddick Bowe in two brutal fights, both of which he lost on fouls. Golota seemed unable to keep his punches above the belt-line even when Bowe was in a helpless position. The Pole was rough, tough and dangerous, and nobody, apart from Lewis, wanted to meet him. Instead of backing off, Lewis went in guns blazing and Golota was soon on the canvas. When he got up, Lewis clubbed him down again and Golota was still trying to get to his feet as the count reached ten. This win led to the unification fight of Lewis v Evander Holyfield in March 1999 that ended in a controversial draw.

Left: Lennox Lewis holds the WBC Heavyweight Championship belt over his head.

Below: Lewis (right) lands a blow to the head of Golota.

NASEEM HAMED V KEVIN KELLEY

December 19 1997
Madison Square Garden, New York

Between them, Hamed and Kelley scored six knockdowns in the brief time that their battle lasted. Hamed was the first to touch down – at the end of the first round – and again in the second. He got up to turn the tables with a left hook. That took the knockdown score to 2–1 in Kelley's favour. Kelley was well on top in the third, but the end was less than three minutes away. In the fourth round Kelley went down hard from a three-punch combination, got up to drop Hamed for a short count and was then sent down by a solid left. He got up as the count reached ten. It was all over. The near sell-out crowd had witnessed a thriller and Hamed was still WBO featherweight champion.

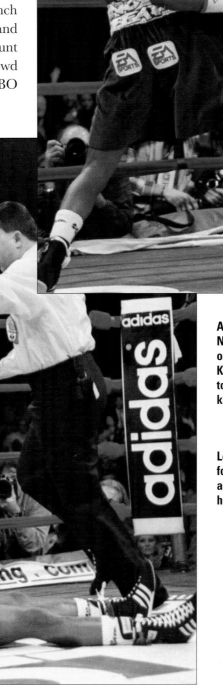

Above: England's Prince Naseem (right) follows through on a punch to the United States' Kevin Kelley, which sent him to the canvas for a fourth round knockout.

Left: Hamed celebrates his fourth round knockout of Kelley, as referee Benji Estaves sends him to a neutral corner.

CARL THOMPSON V
CHRIS EUBANK

April 18 1998 Manchester
July 18 1998 Sheffield

A thrilling first fight drew a capacity crowd for a return match in which Thompson's WBO cruiser-weight title was again at stake. This was even more bitterly contested than the first meeting, and Eubank was ahead going into round eight. It was at this stage that facial damage badly handicapped the challenger. He had been the better man, technically, and had not backed off when it came to fighting toe to toe, but his left eye was closed at the end of the seventh and Thompson went in for the kill. Eubank took some smashing punches and came right back with some of his own. Both showed tremendous commitment to win. It was exciting stuff, but the state of Eubank's eye eventually brought about the referee's intervention. Chris was ahead on points but the bigger man was coming on a fast clip. Thompson won, but in defeat Eubank made himself many friends.

Below: Eubank (right) has slipped inside a left to score with a punch that has also nullified any danger from Thompson's right. The swelling around Eubank's left eye eventually cost him the fight.

OSCAR DE LA HOYA V IKE QUARTEY

February 13 1999
Las Vegas

Two unbeaten fighters, who both rate as being among the best pound-for-pound performers currently operating, clashed in a WBC welterweight title fight and after twelve rounds, the prestige of both remained unimpaired. De La Hoya held on to his title by a split decision but had to climb off the floor to do so. He came back to twice deck the challenger, Ike Quartey from Ghana, but still needed a big last round to clinch the verdict. The see-saw action was at its most tempestuous in round six. Quartey was twice floored but got up to put the champion down and gain a narrow lead. Oscar needed a big last round and mounted a sustained attack. He dropped Quartey briefly, then rallied for two minutes with some terrific punching to put his nose in front. The verdict was hotly disputed, but boxing thrives on controversy and only a rematch will settle the arguments as to who is the better man.

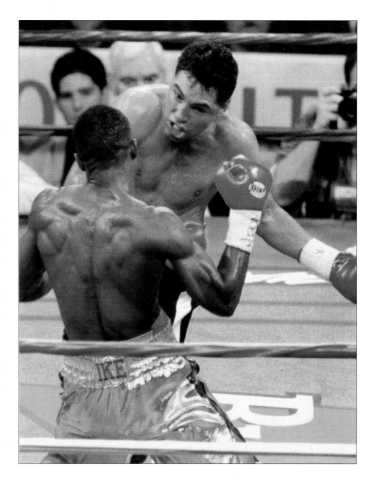

Right: Oscar De La Hoya (right) presses an attack on Ike Quartey of Ghana during the third round of their WBC welterweight title fight.

LENNOX LEWIS V EVANDER HOLYFIELD

November 13 1999
Las Vegas

This fight warrants its inclusion, not because it was a great encounter – it wasn't – but because of the fact that it unified the world heavyweight championship which had been fragmented for nearly a decade. Lewis was defending his WBC title and Holyfield the title recognized by the WBA and IBF.

They had met eight months earlier in New York when a drawn decision had sparked off furious accusations that Lewis had been robbed. The return also went the full distance, but this time Lewis won a unanimous verdict. Holyfield took time to get into the fight then came on to win the middle rounds. Lewis came back to win the last two rounds through good use of his reach and weight advantages. His victory gave Britain its first undisputed world heavyweight champion of the twentieth century.

Above: Lewis scores with an accurate straight left. A shrewd, tactical boxer, he made full use of his physical advantages.

INDEX